UNLEASH

EMPOWERING THE NEXT
GENERATION OF LEADERS

MARV NELSON

ABINGDON PRESS

NASHVILLE

UNLEASH
EMPOWERING THE NEXT GENERATION OF LEADERS

Editor: Chris Folmsbee
Designer: Kent Sneed

All Web addresses were correct and operational at the time of publication.

Print:
ISBN: 9781501844577
PACP10543993-01

Epub:
ISBN: 9781501844584
PACP10543994-01

18 19 20 21 22 23 24 25 26 27—10 9 8 7 6 5 4 3 2 1

MANUFACTURED IN THE UNITED STATES OF AMERICA

For my father, Marvin E. Nelson,
who through his life mentored me more than he knows.
This book is also for the many other mentors who poured
into me, even when it seemed as if I wasn't getting it!

By providing relevant and affordable products and resources, real-time consulting, practical on-site, regional based training and ongoing research, Burlap helps churches of all sizes revitalize their congregations.

Burlap offers hope-based solutions to reach millennials and generation Z throughout the entire scope of its work throughout North America. We can help your church navigate the changing cultural landscape by discovering already-existing assets within your church and community to create new stories of hope and renewal.

burlap

www.ThinkBurlap.com

CONTENTS

PREFACE

In my second church, when I met the pastor I reported to, his first words to me were, "I want to know you, Marv." He then asked me to take a series of tests and to read through two books—*StrengthsFinder 2.0* by Tom Rath and *Who Moved My Cheese?* by Spencer Johnson. He said to me, "Once you go through all of those tasks and we discuss it together, I will know you well." He wasn't lying. As a leader, John put much stock in the power of leading well, which follows the idea of *knowing* well. John passionately pursued knowing his staff so that he could best lead them and direct them toward achieving their purpose. Little did I know how this "knowing" process would lead to an equipping and releasing season in my life. I thought I had myself pegged as a youth pastor for life, but John and several other mentors in my life saw something different within me and for me.

Three years into my time at Allegheny Center Alliance Church (ACAC) as the middle school youth pastor, I felt a tug at my heart to do something different. When I felt God's call to lead ACAC's college campus plant, I went directly to John. I shared the call, and he simply said, "I was wondering when you'd come around." John knew I would fit this position perfectly, but waited for me to come to a place of self-knowledge. John and my managing pastor, Scott, would go on to make and take the necessary time to equip me and ultimately release me into this new, never-been-done-before (by ACAC) position as campus plant pastor. I felt completely unleashed for lifelong leadership and kingdom impact. I am an older millennial, and I believe fully that the formula that was modeled for me (unknowingly at the time, I might add) was the best formula possible for leading emerging leaders.

Scores of books, reports, studies, blogs, and articles have been written about the millennial generation and the generation after them—generation Z. Much of the data is at least semicorrect, but many times that data is merely numbers on a page and the people behind those numbers get forgotten or neglected. Rather than getting to know the people behind the numbers, many of today's leaders automatically assume they know (due to the data) how to engage the next generations. This further divides the generations into separate camps, so to speak, and causes the transition or handing over leadership roles and responsibilities much more difficult than it needs to be.

I've heard many church leaders air their frustrations about the millennial generation. Many times, they see next generations as whimsical, self-absorbed, whiny, and unwilling to remain planted where they land. It's as though these leaders are asking, "How can we work with and invest in transient, entitled young people? We've seen data that backs up our ideas about them, and we do not like what we see. They are always trying to get ahead without putting in the work."

Perhaps as you are reading this, you can relate to the leaders I've talked to. I've had these very same quandaries as I work with emerging generations. I've seen some of these negative qualities emerge in many of the millennials I work with, and even in myself, an older millennial at thirty-three. The data on these issues isn't untrue. The numbers aren't lying. Yet they do not tell the whole story either. Some of the most oft-quoted research data on millennials came from a 2013 *Time* magazine article titled "Millennials: The Me Me Me Generation."[1] Although the data is remembered, some of the key components from the article explaining why millennials are important and what good they bring to the table are forgotten. Many leaders simply take the data at face value. They take note when a millennial acts in a way that proves the data, but many times they fail to know the person behind the data.

There are other numbers we're not looking at—numbers that Burlap has been uncovering—insightful, unpredictable realities of these generations that many are failing to applaud or even recognize.[2] The data and numbers that many of us look at cause trepidation for the future. Many current Silent Generation, boomers, and Xer leaders wonder what's to become of the church, our nation, and our world in the hands of emerging generations. With so much fear, there are fewer leadership handoffs—older leaders seem unwilling to hand off certain aspects of leadership to younger leaders. The older generations' leaders are acting as quarterbacks, if you will, and they are holding the ball and not throwing it or pitching it to the emerging generation. Sooner or later, the linebacker is coming in for the sack. The leaders of today will always have to hand off the ball to the emerging leaders of future generations in order to have sustainability and effectiveness. This is true in any generation, not just the ones we see emerging now. How can we effectively lead in such a way that we set up the right play and throw the ball at the right time in order to score?

I believe that effectively setting up strong future leaders takes three things. The first of these is *knowing*. As I stated above, the people behind the numbers are being neglected. Many times, assumptions and stereotypes are assumed before relationships are even made. The fear of throwing the ball to the emerging generation comes down to not knowing them enough to trust them. Even if we are "spending time" with emerging generations, are we really getting to *know* them, or are we watching them to see if they fit into the assumptions we've made about them based on the data we've read? The research is important, but the people behind the research *need* to be known and made more important than the data. Being known for who they are and not who we assume them to be is a passionate desire of emerging generations.

If we're honest, it's a desire of ours as well. We all have a desire to know and be known (we will unpack this biblically and psychologically in the upcoming chapters). This book will walk through the art of knowing this generation. We will walk together through the basis for this need, as well as ways in which to engage these generations in the art of knowing. The great news is that as you get to know the people you lead, they will also get to know *you*. This knowing will set up impetus for the rest of the book. Without it—knowing, that is—trust can't be formed enough to walk through the other two aspects of equipping and releasing. You must know them and they must know you to move forward.

Equipping is the second piece necessary for empowering the emerging generation of leaders. Once there is mutual trust, we can then equip young leaders with the skills and knowledge they need to be successful leaders. Due to their wisdom, tenured leaders have a lot to offer younger men and women who desire to lead. These emerging generations are hungry for the wisdom of these seasoned leaders. That may come as a shock to you and that might be because you have read too much into the data and have not spent enough time *with* millennials or generation Z. In my experience, one of the main values emerging generations want from older generations is mentorship. Younger leaders may not always know the best ways to articulate this or know how to go about it, but they most certainly want it and recognize they need it. If emerging leaders know you and trust you, they will likely see your faithful and fruitful leadership and want to learn from you. Once you know them, you will see where they need equipping and you will have earned the right to speak into their lives.

I will share five key issues that all future leaders need (no matter their generation) and how to go about equipping them in these five aspects. Yet we cannot come from a place of assumption. It helps if leaders can lead or guide those in the emerging generations into the areas they need to grow in rather than pulling them and dragging them into them. The five key issues I will unpack are character, influence, vision, communication, and surrender. In my own leadership experience with the younger generations, these five aspects are vital to their growth, as well as to the health of those they will lead. Jesus himself encouraged his disciples in these five areas, and so I think it is of utmost importance we do the same.[3]

The third and final aspect of unleashing emerging generations into leadership is *releasing*. It's one thing to discuss the how-tos and a completely different thing to take action on them. The third part of this book will give the action steps. After we've poured into, grown, taught, made into disciples, mentored, and passed on all the wisdom we possibly can, there comes the time for letting the emerging generation take the ball. As current leaders who are called to empower future leaders, it is our job to hand off the ball, turn the plays over to the new quarterback, and get out of the game. We will look at the four ways I have found to best release the leadership to the emerging generations: (1) calling them to flourish, (2) handing over our influence to them, (3) giving them the keys, and finally, (4) getting out of the car and letting them drive away.

Let me say, too, this is *not* merely a book about succession from the main or senior leader to the next main or senior leader. Although aspects of this book can be applied to such a situation, that is not the overarching intent of this book. There are many great books on that topic alone; for example, check out *Next* by my friend Warren Bird and coauthor William Vanderbloemen.

This book is about unleashing the emerging generation of leaders into all types of leadership roles, such as directors, department heads, managers, and the like. This book also encourages giving young leaders the freedom to dream up new roles that will need a uniquely developed leader. There may be some leadership roles in your organization that need to be adjusted or roles you need that only a young leader could dream up. This book is also about confidently and expectantly handing over the future of the church to young elders, deacons, and yes, even lead pastors. Given the current ecclesial climate and landscape, this book is needed and needed right now. *Relevant* magazine recently stated in an article titled, "Where Are All of the Millennial Pastors?" that the average age of senior pastors in 1991 was forty-four, while as of 2016, the average age of pastors was fifty-four.[4] We need younger leaders now. Not because the kingdom of God is ever in trouble, but because the next generation needs to be set up for the best possible opportunity to spread the good news of the Kingdom.

Finally, before we dive into the depths of this book, let me say that this book is also about belief, a confident and expectant belief in the emerging generations of leaders. This is a belief that is convinced, confident, unconflicted, and unwavering in its trust in the emerging generation. When we can come to this type of belief, we can help them also believe in themselves.

One emerging leader whom I have had the pleasure of working with is Joseph Wimer. He has been with me since the inception of our campus plant at the University of Pittsburgh. I've spent many years working alongside him and implementing many of the concepts I explain in this book to know, grow, and equip him as a leader. My belief in Joseph is unwavering. I once told him, "Joseph, if I die tomorrow, I am not worried about Aletheia. I know you could lead this campus plant and lead it well." This is the type of belief I write this book with—one that is convinced of the capabilities, passion, and power of the emerging generation.

UNLEASH is a book about the belief that God desires the best for the church today and for the church tomorrow and for the church always. It is critical that we all begin this journey of gifting leadership to emerging generations in a spirit of belief. We must believe in the emerging generations. We must have hope and optimism rather than a doom-and-gloom type of pessimism. Let us all leave those feelings of dread at the door and look to a bright future with godly, passionate leaders who will lead that future.

Part 1
The Art of Knowing

CHAPTER 1

NO MASKS ALLOWED

*Our masks have become our reality, and we have become our lies. In short,
we have lost authenticity and adopted an identity based on illusion.
We have become a house of smoke and mirrors.*
—David Benner, The Gift of Being Yourself[5]

*I am the good shepherd. I know my own and my own know me, just as the Father
knows me and I know the Father. (John 10:14-15, ESV)*

ONE OF THE COLLEGE STUDENTS IN MY ministry discovered the power of being known this semester. She is one of those happy-go-lucky, Disney-princess-loving type of girls. She always has a happy face on and constantly jokes around with everyone in our campus church. During one of our services, I was preaching a message on taking our masks off. The main point of the message was to challenge our students to be honest with themselves, and others, with their struggles, sins, fears, doubts, and pain. During the sermon, I gave a description of my past issues with a pornography addiction and how I hid behind a mask to cover up my sin. I was studying to be a pastor, and I felt compelled to hide behind a mask of "good future pastor" because in my mind, pastors never struggled with things like this.

After the service, she took me aside and began to let me in on some of the big issues in her life. She was struggling with alcohol and partying and had recently received a citation for underage drinking. She told me that my vulnerability helped her be vulnerable as well. Ever since that Sunday, she's been on a journey of demasking herself. She's been insanely honest with one of our staff members about many more issues in her life. She has seen the true love of God from people who truly know her and has stepped into leadership roles at our church as a result. The genesis for this was a simple choice of authenticity by a leader she respected and trusted. Taking off our masks not only helps propel those around us to know us, but it also gives others the freedom to be known as well because they will feel free to take their masks off too. Emerging generations see demasking as a desperate need—and as leaders of emerging leaders, we must learn this and apply it.

This principle is not just helpful; it's biblical. When God created humanity, God designed them with two innate desires—two desires God shares with humans—to know and be known. You can see this truth immediately in God's relationship with Adam. God created Adam, spent time with Adam, and discovered through knowing Adam that something was missing. God then created Eve to fill that missing piece, as well as to display a fuller picture of who God is. We are all created in the image of God (the Imago Dei), and so this image of community, intimacy, and relationship—knowing and being known—is supremely important to the completion of the Imago Dei. In this one masterful event of love, God displayed God's knowing of Adam and God's own desire to be more fully known by God's creation.

The desire to be known and to know continues throughout the Genesis story. God walked together in the garden with Adam and Eve. Through time and activity together, the three of them grew in their knowledge of one another. Genesis 2:25 describes the most beautiful explanation of this knowing. The Scripture says that Adam and Eve were both naked and unashamed.

Nothing hidden. No masks. No secrets. No pretending. Just pure, simple, honest communion and partnership that created an environment in which the whole of their selves was completely exposed to God, and to one another, without any fear of rejection or insecurity. This is the type of knowing we all crave. Deep within us, we long for a place where the fear of rejection for who we really are can be forever expelled. We will never get back to the garden of Eden, but we can begin to experience aspects of this type of honest community. In this, we can have a taste of the final garden in the middle of the city of God that we read about in Revelation 21 and 22. There, we will return to a garden in which there will be no more hiding. As leaders who lead current and future leaders, we have an opportunity to develop what I call cultures of knowing. I believe we must develop these types of cultures everywhere we live, work, and play, especially within the church community. I would suggest that if we do not create these cultures, we will pass up many future leaders, leaving them unknown and, therefore, further disillusioned with the church or maybe even leadership in general.

When we study the constant barrage of data before us on the millennial generation as well as on generation Z, we can see a recognizable pattern of thought as it pertains to the church. The pattern of thought is that churches are largely viewed as judgmental and fake. The first research effort from the Barna Group that discovered the severity of the millennial generation's disdain for the church in these areas was written ten years ago and published in a book titled *UnChristian: What a New Generation Really Thinks About Christianity . . . and Why It Matters*. These sentiments have only been reinforced over the last ten years and have been picked up by the generation emerging behind millennials. I confess, as an older millennial and a pastor, I too have experienced both judgmental and hypocritical attributes from more churched people than unchurched.

A masked culture is one in which the majority of people are actors playing a part. They show up, act as they know they're supposed to, say the right things, display the right image, but deep down they know little of it is real for them. They can't share when they don't feel like showing up. They can't be honest if they're doubting internally. They can't frown when they're expected to smile, and they can't admit when they mess up due to the fear of rejection. So, the play continues.

This does not have to be the case moving into the future. I believe this is a church culture issue and that culture is developed primarily through the leaders. As leaders, we have a chance to change the fake, mask-wearing culture that plagues the Christian culture and hinders our ability to speak into the lives of the emerging generation. It begins with us. We can no longer lead as leaders who fail to be known and who fail at knowing those we are seeking to grow as leaders.

"What kind of pastor do you want to be?" That question rang in my ears when it was first asked of me. I was in college, studying to be in ministry, and I desperately wanted to be a great pastor. Who goes to school for a specific realm of leadership and wants to be bad at it? For that matter, who wants to be mediocre? I sure didn't. So, I gave my answer aloud to the person asking the question: "I want to be a great pastor."

The response I received in return to my answer was blunt, offensive (to me at least), and unnerving. The response was this: "Then you need counseling . . ." I felt as though a truck had hit me. My calm, confident, and yet arrogantly put-together self began to crumble that day. It was the start of a journey I am still on to this day—a journey of trying to become unmasked and a journey toward living in such a way that is naked and unashamed (Genesis 2:25). I had to face the fact that

I was not who I thought I was. I had to allow the Spirit of God to reveal my true self and, therefore, give me the ability to truly be known by others.

Do you want to be a great leader?

Do you want to be a leader who leaves a legacy of leaders behind to do your job even better than you did?

Of course you do, or you would not be reading this book.

Since it is true, my first piece of advice is to begin the journey of being unmasked and letting yourself be known. Don't hide behind supposed perfection. Be honest about doubts, fears, and struggles. Stop covering up your mistakes with excuses. Apologize when you've wounded someone. Share past failures to more completely humanize yourself.

How does this connect to knowing our young leaders? How does this help develop relationships of knowing? In any relationship, it is easy to put on a mask or a false self that we think the other person would like for us to be. It can be tempting because we can shape a person who is respected, strong, well-liked, and gregarious, even if that is not our real self. We can portray a self that is anything we want it to be, as long as we are good enough actors. We do this because it works to some degree, at least for a while. People end up liking our false self, so we continue to project our false self. The false self lurks around the corner in every relationship, including our relationship to God and even the relationship we have with ourselves.

The problem with our masks is that they cause us to go through life not fully being *known*. We all have an intrinsic lasting desire to *know* others and be *known* by others. It was implanted in us at Creation and will remain within us for eternity, from garden to garden. We long for the garden experience of being naked and unashamed, yet fear this type of exposure because there is a real possibility of rejection and this creates within us myriad insecurities. The garden resonates with each one of us, as author and pastor Chris Folmsbee so aptly put it.[6] There may have been times of openness in our lives that ended up biting us in the end, and so we told ourselves that we would never allow this to happen again. As leaders, we may even have a stronger fear of our openness coming back to bite us with those who follow us. This attitude or outlook, however, fortifies the masks we wear.

The problem with our masks in leadership is that they create a leadership style that is inauthentic and detached from healthy relationships. It causes the environments we lead to have the same detached, inauthentic community. When young leaders enter places with this type of inauthentic culture, they bristle and are therefore hard to mentor and guide. They will see the environment as judgmental and hypocritical, not welcoming and open. They will not open up their soul, and a growing, deep, and intimate relationship will be tough to cultivate.

The people we lead may generally see within us a confident, all-knowing leader and rarely see anything else. When problems arise, we can react with our assumptions and neglect the real issues. We may not like being told we are wrong, and we rarely admit failures. When others (especially young leaders) bring ideas to the table, we easily dismiss them because it doesn't fit "our plan." We may rework certain plans repeatedly, but won't admit when we need help, even though it is painfully obvious to everyone that we need it. This is inauthentic, mask-wearing leadership.

None of us is immune to the temptations of this type of leadership style. Many leaders I've worked with and under have struggled with this, as have I. I remember an event idea I had for our campus church. I thought it was a perfect idea. I tossed the event idea to the team, thinking it was a home run. Not one person on the team rallied behind it. I pushed it through anyway, and we had little to no people show up. I didn't listen. I didn't ask for help. I shrugged off ideas because I felt I needed to be confident in my event plan. I learned the hard way that leading in that way was a hindrance, rather than a help.

Many reading this may be taken aback because, after all, aren't we trained to be confident? Aren't we as leaders supposed to have the answers? The answer, of course, is both yes and no. As leaders, we are called to lead, and we should not be constantly wavering on the directions in which we are leading the people following us. Yet we should live in the realm of simple honesty. Part of dropping or taking off our mask is being honest. When we mess up, we fess up. When we aren't sure of the plan going forward, we say so and joyfully seek input from our team. After all, who really wants to follow a phony who doesn't admit mistakes? Being authentic is admitting when we've messed up. It's asking forgiveness for those mistakes, and it's holding others to a standard of authenticity as well. Emerging generations are fed up with pretentious and counterfeit leaders everywhere: in the church, in politics, and in major corporations. They are done with the fake and desire real, raw authenticity. LifeWay conducted a study of millennials in 2014 that opened everyone's eyes to the full reality of the millennials' disdain for inauthentic leadership. In the findings section of this study, Thom Rainer said,

"They don't want phony; they want authentic. They don't want pretentious; they want transparent."[7] Leaders who pretend to have all the right answers are easily discovered and seen as fake by the emerging generations.

Exposing doubts and struggles and honestly stating they don't know something poses a huge problem for most leaders because they've been trained to have the answers and to be strong, confident, and have no weak links in their armor. Even as pastors, many of us have been trained to share very little from our true self, and when we do, we share a success story, not a failure story.

Leaders everywhere must unlearn this harmful training if they ever expect people of younger generations to follow them over the long haul. As leaders, we must learn, relearn, and practice the ancient art of repentance and confession, a lesson that sadly many pastors struggle with on a large scale. When a leader offers confession and repentance, the emerging generation will take notice and respect that leader more than if they hadn't experienced it. We must consistently check ourselves and ensure we live confessional lives among our emerging generation followers. King Saul is a leader in the Bible with much to teach us. His failures in leadership largely stemmed from his consistent and effective mask-wearing.

Remember, this book is not a "leadership" book on how leaders need to learn new "leadership skills." The purpose of this book is far different from that. The purpose of this book is to give you insight on how to *know, equip,* and *release* younger, emerging leaders. Although this book's purpose is different, I think we can see biblical examples of failed leadership and learn from them.

I remember a time when a congregant gently corrected me on a minor issue. I had said something wrong in a sermon. I simply made an error about a biblical story. It wasn't heretical, but it was a mistake. They felt the need to point it out so if I preach that sermon again, I could make the necessary adjustment. In the heat of the moment, I told the college student, "Well, it can be interpreted two different ways. I simply gave the lesser known way of interpretation." As soon as I said it, I knew what I was saying wasn't true and so did the student I was telling it to. I had a choice—own my lie and apologize for the mistake in the sermon or keep the "I'm right" statement. Thankfully, the Holy Spirit immediately convicted me, and I confessed to both mistakes. If I hadn't, not only would I have been in sin, but I also would've lost the confidence of that student.

When things go bad, it's easy to point the finger and say, "The board wouldn't allow me to make changes" or "The church members are too old to move, so we stayed stagnant" or "I have too many office hours to fill, so I don't spend time in the community." Leaders must own problems, especially in front of the younger leaders they hope to one day unleash into areas and positions of future leadership. If all these young leaders hear is a story that failure belongs to everyone else and not us as leaders, they will only see counterfeit leadership.

However, when the people we lead see us owning up to our failures, they can feel free to own up to theirs. However, if we neglect to own it, it won't change because we'll continue to sweep it under the carpet and pretend it doesn't exist. Good leaders who unleash other leaders own their failures and seek to make it right.

Over the years I have spent in ministry, I repeatedly found that vulnerability produces greater levels of vulnerability in all of us. Therefore, I've intentionally spent time in this book to share how leaders can take off our "leader mask." If we truly want to know the younger leaders we hope to unleash, we must first give them opportunity to know us. It's not just in moments of confession or admitting when we're wrong, although those are great starting points. It's allowing younger leaders to share our fears, doubts, and struggles, as well as triumphs and wins. When we live with no masks allowed, we create a culture of mask-less leading, and people, particularly the younger leaders around us, can start to be truly known.

As stated before, this generation is crying out for real, raw, transparent leadership. If leaders leave this on the side of the road and treat it as if it is another "meaningless leadership fad," they will continue to lose ground with this generation. Many people making up the emerging generations are longing to be free from the enslavement that wearing masks can bring. Those in the emerging generation may not articulate this well, but their cry for authenticity is a cry to be accepted *as they are.* The cry of emerging generations is to get back to the original reality of humanity—naked and unashamed. I believe this longing is the driving force behind many of the social issues we find these generations fighting for, particularly as it pertains to the LGBTQ community (lesbian, gay, bisexual, transgender, queer or questioning). There is a demand for everyone to be included in a safe environment that exposes and highlights who they really are, without fear of rejection. If we're going to speak into the lives of emerging generations, they must trust us. In order for millennials and generation Z to trust us, they need to know we *know* them and they *know* us, but it begins with us allowing ourselves to be known.

This type of transparent leadership isn't easy, and it's hard to know how transparent we need to be. This is where we as Christian leaders must seek to be led by the power and guidance of the Holy Spirit. We must first let ourselves be known by God and seek to know God as well. This type of knowing is transformational and encourages deeper dependence upon the Lord and less upon us. I encourage you to take time to read a small book that will help you by leaps and bounds in knowing and being known by God. The book is written by David G. Benner and entitled, *The Gift of Being Yourself: The Sacred Call to Self-Discovery*. David is a Christian psychologist who uncovers the issue of our need to be known and to know others. When God knows us, it becomes a lot easier to spot our self-endorsed masks and then to let down our masks, so we can allow ourselves to be truly known by others as well. This type of authenticity sounds scary—because it is. To some, it might even sound antithetical to leading well. However, I can assure you with certainty based on experiences that in the emerging generation, authenticity is a highly valued commodity and will propel your ability to mentor, guide, make into disciples, and unleash them in ways other types of leadership practices can't.

Once we have cultivated a safe environment for people to truly be known, we have to be ready for what will inevitably come. The flood of honest confessions can be quite overwhelming. In attempting to lead with transparency, many of my young leaders have exposed some serious issues that guide and direct their lives that conflict with God's intentions for their lives. I learned the hard way that to keep a mask-less culture, my immediate reactions to their confessions are critical. When I get to know them on this deeper level of knowing, I *can't* reject them. They know the standard I adhere to and the gospel we as a church teach, so they are aware of where I stand on the issues that conflict with a life marked by the virtues of Jesus. I don't need to tell them, but I do need to help them. *When young leaders are struggling, we must come alongside them.*

When we truly know the younger leaders in our midst and walk with them in the struggles they invite us into, they will trust us. When they trust us, we can speak into their lives. We can no longer just assume we know what those we are leading need. We need to know them enough to know what they need and even lovingly help them know what they need. By living in our masks so long, we will think that's who we really are. George MacDonald once said, "Half of the misery in the world comes from trying to *look*, instead of trying to *be*, what one is not."[8]

When it comes to authenticity, you can't put up a front. You can't *look* authentic. You have to *be* authentic. If we as leaders are not authentic, we will only cause misery with the younger leaders around us. This art of knowing, as I call it, will be the catalyst for growth and will give us the confidence and trust to release leadership responsibilities over to them.

Many young leaders don't feel known, and because of this, they don't feel trusted or that they can trust someone else. Many times, older leaders don't trust them because we don't know them, or we assume we know them and often we don't like what we see. Making assumptions about them and either pretending or falsely appearing that we know them drives them away. With emerging generations, we must *never* assume we know them or the way they'd lead given a particular set of circumstances or a specific situation. We must take the time to know and be known.

Finally, when we truly know the young leaders in our midst, we will find ourselves pleasantly surprised. Although much of the data collected about emerging generations is correct, the way in which it has been skewed and poorly presented is staggering. Once we get to actually know the people behind the data, we will find that although there are struggles (as with any generation) with emerging generations, there is much to be hopeful about. They get things we as older leaders don't. They see things we can't. They may see roadblocks to their generation in a particular vision plan or quickly understand different cultural nuances we as older leaders can easily miss. They can see how to bring certain ideas or messages to the attention of our current culture in ways we simply don't understand. They can easily get a glimpse of how to engage certain topics with grace and sensitivity that we as leaders may be blind to.

When we allow ourselves to be consumed with the disheartening data that gets thrown out and about recklessly regarding millennials and generation Z, we are inclined to lose hope. This hopelessness sadly causes us to cling to places of leadership that we should be relinquishing and can feed the strife between the generations. When we get to know the future leaders around us, I guarantee we will find cause for hope.

The future of the church, our nonprofit organization, or our businesses isn't as bleak as some of the experts may project. The way the emerging generations will choose to shape our churches and our businesses, once they lead them, will look different, but they won't be the disaster we may be anticipating. We *will* reignite our hope for the future once we truly take time to know those behind the numbers.

This doesn't mean we won't disagree. This doesn't mean that it won't be a grind. This doesn't even mean we should change the way we see the future direction of the roles in which we lead. What it does mean is this: *the world does not end when we step down from leadership* or hand over areas of leadership to the younger generations. Things will be different, but those things will not be disasters. Trusting the emerging generation to be unleashed will still be difficult when we get to really know them, but we will see the future in a more hopeful light. Let us then lead in the art of going first. May we seek to be known by those we lead, so we can better know them and begin to reignite our hope for the future leaders we will unleash.

In the chapters that follow in part 1, we will see how we can better get to know the emerging generations in real, deep, and rich ways. These chapters will each outline ways we can best facilitate the art of knowing with those we hope to unleash for ministry impact. The first way to facilitate knowing is by asking good questions. As you will see, the questions we ask the current and future leaders we are mentoring can ultimately result in developing rapport, developing a foundational friendship in which to build upon and, finally, allowing us to deeply know the people whose lives we are shaping in order to unleash them for high-impact, sustainable, and faithful ministry and leadership.

CHAPTER 2

THE NEED FOR QUESTIONS

The quality of a leader cannot be judged by the answers he gives,
but by the questions he asks.
—Simon Sinek[9]

But the LORD God called to the man and said to him: "Where are you?"
(Genesis 3:9, ESV)

WHEN WE ARE SEEKING TO KNOW SOMEONE, something, or someplace, we usually begin with questions. One year I experienced this in a very intense way from a college freshman. He asked if we could go to lunch after the first Sunday because he had a few questions. Once we sat down for lunch, a string of questions came pouring out of this young man. He wanted to know everything from orthodoxy (what we believe) to orthopraxis (how we practice that which we believe). He grilled me with question after question. Afterward, he simply said, "Yeah, I think this is a church I can really be a part of." His goal? To know. He wanted to know me as a pastor, what I stood for and how I went about living out what I believed. He wanted to know the church. Would he be comfortable? Would he feel able to be himself? Questions fuel knowing. This chapter takes that idea, blows it up, and explains how to do it well.

In the garden, after the Fall occurred, God reestablished God's desire to be known by and to know Adam and Eve. God began this with a question. This is after they had run away and hidden themselves. God pursued them in their hiding and offered a question to draw them out of hiding. God knew where Adam and Eve were. God knew why they hid. Yet God still pursued. Despite what I said about millennials and gen Z in the previous chapter wanting to be known, they still fear it like anyone else. It's easier to hide. It's easier to cover up. It is easier to hold back some of who we really are in order to project who we want people to think we are. This takes a pursuit on our part (those of us leading these young leaders). Let's face facts—there is a load of distrust between generations. There has been a track record of running away from and ignoring one another—or at the very least, dismissing one another's perspective and outlook on life. For the church (and any other organization, really) to avoid being hindered in the future, the generations must come together and come together *now*. Leaders must choose to go first. Going first shows maturity. Going first offers a hand where it was assumed there wasn't one. Going first shows humility.

Going first also shows a search is in progress. We cannot miss the importance of the emerging generations' need for being pursued or for us to search for who they truly are and want to become. To those in the emerging generations, being valued, for many at least, is best expressed by being sought out. The Lord Jesus himself pursued humankind through the Incarnation. Following the example of Jesus can never be wrong. Jesus will never stunt efforts to be like him. Choosing to pursue is seeking out those in the emerging generations and beginning with questions. When we go first in this endeavor to know, it will say to this generation: "You matter to me. Who you are matters to me." Those in the emerging generation will feel highly valued. It will open a door of sharing with them and knowing them that wouldn't be there without this first effort of pursuit.

If we are to lead the way in closing the generational gaps, we must choose to go first. Going first can be as simple as opening up about failures and as deep as confessing sins that are hindering you in your leadership. Going first would be admitting when you're wrong and being the first to agree with the person who holds you accountable. This type of going first will lead to deep trust from the emerging generations and will give older leaders a leg up in developing the young leaders who surround them.

I've talked with many boomers who complain about millennials. They throw the widely distributed data and stats around like a joke and enjoy doing it at times. This unhealthy practice reveals a lack of *knowing*. As leaders who are seeking to lead and unleash the emerging generations, we've got to be the ones who suck it up and pursue—taking the first step. God pursues us. God knows everything about us. It is simply God's nature. However, God doesn't sit in heaven or pace around complaining about us. God doesn't use God's knowledge of us as an excuse to walk away. God knew what Adam and Eve had done and still didn't walk away. God went after Adam and Eve in a spirit of love and affection. God wanted to have them remain in charge of creation. God desired Adam and Eve to flourish and thrive. This should be the same attitude with which leaders approach the young leaders in our midst. Leaders should reject the idea of hopelessness with this generation. It doesn't matter what leaders think they know about the emerging generations; leaders must pursue the emerging generation with a godly desire to see them flourish.

In this pursuit, the way we approach younger leaders is everything. We may try to pursue in ways that we were pursued—with cold, hard facts. We may seek to give "just the facts" (to quote an old TV show, *Dragnet*) and nothing more. Yet the way in which we approach the younger generations can't be the approach we would take with older generations. This is where the need for questions comes into play. We must pursue with an attitude of love and curiosity. Nothing is more valuable to this generation than leaders admitting they don't have it all together and don't know everything. When we ask questions, we reveal we don't have all the answers. If you want to know your young leaders and want to be able to be confident in handing leadership over to them when you're gone, begin with questions.

In the art of knowing, questions are essential. Edgar Schein, in his book *Humble Inquiry*, says, "There is growing evidence that many tasks get accomplished better and more safely if team members and especially bosses learn to build relationships through the art of Humble Inquiry."[10] Inquiry is how we best build a relationship. Schein goes on to say, "We also live in a structured society in which building relationships is not as important as task accomplishment, in which it is appropriate and expected that the subordinate does more asking than telling, while the boss does more telling than asking. Having to ask is a sign of weakness or ignorance, so we avoid it as much as possible."[11]

Think of a first date. Asking and answering questions likely takes up most of the time together on that first date. Why? Because questions seek to bring about knowledge of the person who is answering our questions. There is a desire to know if the person is a good fit for us, so we ask specific, detailed questions so we can dig deep into who that person is. On this first date, we may observe behaviors and then ask a series of important questions based on our observations. We will, in turn, respond or answer questions that reveal who we are to the other. We don't start off a first date declaring how the person across the table from us should act, think, or love. If we did, the date would end before it even began. Questions bring about a deeper sense of knowing. Good questions bring about an even better sense of knowing. Simply put, the agenda for questions is to know.

In our relationships with the future leaders among us, the same is true. Questions are essential for our getting to know them. We must seek to ask good, hard questions. This seems obvious, doesn't it? Yet many leaders who lead younger leaders today fail at asking good questions or fail to even ask questions at all. For many older leaders, the goal of relationship with the younger generation is simply knowledge transference. This type of leader doesn't care about the person per se; they want to know the person "gets it" and will do as the leader desires or complete the tasks assigned. Many times, the "knowledge transference" type of leader doesn't want to learn anything from the emerging leader, but simply wants to pass on their great wisdom. This hinders the teachability of the leader and begins to put a wall between the older leader and the emerging leader.

I've discovered that many leaders are even less inclined to answer or respond to good, hard questions when younger leaders ask them. It is often wrongly assumed that the younger generations' questions are coming from a place of insubordination or a lack of respect or a desire to challenge, rather than from a place of humble curiosity. This type of leader most likely won't even leave much room to be asked questions by the younger leaders under their leadership. If we desire the younger leaders, whom we hope to unleash, to trust us, we must be willing to answer their questions as well. One of the biggest questions I receive from the emerging generation leaders around me is the question, "Why?" When I share where I feel we should go as a church or as a ministry, the "Why?" question always occurs. It's hard not to view this as a pushback, but many times it is a simple inquiry so there can be a deeper understanding by those younger. Many in the emerging generation have experienced the age-old answer—"Because I said so"—but this will no longer be enough. When I take time to field questions such as "Why?" I find my younger leaders are more eager to get after the "what."

Jesus knew this. He was a master at asking questions and took time to answer questions as well (even if the answers were sometimes cryptic). In fact, Jesus asked 307 recorded questions. Two such questions come in Matthew 16, where he asked his disciples, "Who is everyone saying I am?" Then he followed up their answer with, "Who do *you* say I am?" He went right to the heart of the issue and challenged his disciples to make a claim on his true identity. He wanted them to be aware of who they thought he was, and he wanted them to admit to him whom they thought they were following. I'm betting he asked many more questions that were not recorded. Asking questions was not only his way of getting to know his disciples, but it was also his main form of teaching the disciples. Jesus would intentionally ask specific, hard, and pointed questions to draw his hearers to the nuggets of truth he wanted them to grasp.

Why didn't Jesus avoid the first step of asking the questions and simply come out and declare what he wanted his disciples to know? I believe it's because Jesus wanted to get them hungrier to learn. He wanted to lead them to the answer and have a passionate desire to know it. He drew them in. He grabbed their attention. He made them feel that they had to know the answer. Sometimes Jesus left them hanging and left them to figure it out on their own, and sometimes he provided them with the answer. In Mark 4:1-20, we see Jesus explaining not only the parable he just told, but also explaining why he spoke in parables and questions. After Jesus asked questions, he would explain the answers to his confused disciples and the conclusions he wanted them to reach. In Luke 20:9-18, we see Jesus ask a question and give what seems like an answer, but even his answer clearly confuses the listener. Just like Jesus, leaders of today can know their young leaders better. As the emerging leaders begin to know their leaders better, we as leaders can leverage the questions they ask to grow, challenge, mold, and unleash them. I'll call these two aspects of the importance of asking questions *knowing* and *growing*.

Knowing

Questions should be used to *know* our young leaders. Edgar Schein defines this type of inquiry well: "The kind of inquiry I am talking about derives from an attitude of interest and curiosity. It implies a desire to build a relationship that will lead to more open communication."[12] We can use the genius of questions for the purpose of knowing the young leaders in our midst. We need good questions so we can see the real persons, rather than the false faces they may seek to present. Let me share a bit of my experience.

For me, this idea of asking good questions began when I was in college and was asked a very important, deep, revealing question by one of my mentors and friends—Dr. Ron Walborn, now the dean of Alliance Theological Seminary. One day he asked these questions: "Who are the people, where are the places, and what are the things that nourish the life of God within you? Then answer: who are the people, where are the places, and what are the things that choke off the life of God within you?"

These two questions forced me to look at my life, my relationship with God, and things that both hindered and helped me in my walk with Jesus. It took time to be honest, to think about these things, but eventually they came, and I was shocked at the self-revelation that occurred. Dr. Walborn didn't assume he knew my struggles or my areas of success. He didn't presume to know all about me. He genuinely wanted me to know myself and then reveal myself. This truly was a pivotal moment in my life, as it began a continued relationship with a mentor who would ask thoughtful, probing questions that helped me know and reveal my true self. Yes, I could've faked it, but I knew that Ron was providing a safe place for me to be honest. I knew he cared about me. Therefore, I chose to be honest (more on being safe in a moment).

Not only has this technique of asking good questions helped me to reveal myself and be known, but it has also helped me to know those I am leading and ultimately seek to unleash one day. Every Monday night, I gather with young men. These men are men I have selected and hope to unleash (and some of whom are already unleashed) for significant leadership. We gather together, and each Monday I simply ask one question that we all (myself included) answer. Each week, we dig a little deeper into one another's lives and get to know one another better than most men know each other in today's video game society. With these young men, we began our second or third time together with this question: *What are all the sins you can remember committing?*

I can see your face right now. You are probably stunned that I would start a group of young male leaders off with this type of question. So, let me back up and explain why we began to meet in the first place. A talented young man named Alex, who used to be one of the middle school students at the church I serve at, came over to my house. He shared with me his desire for a deeper relationship with God. He described a desire for a gathering of Christian men where he could be known for who he really is and not feel forced to put on a mask. The gathering would certainly allow him and the others to take off any masks they already wore. He shared his desire to be a better leader in the church and in his Christian walk. So, we set out after that night to gather young men with the same desire. Let me simply say here that in my personal experience, young leaders within the millennial and gen Z generations deeply desire spaces such as this. Many can sense a longing for this type of environment, but few find it and even fewer find it in the church.[13]

Alex and I easily found more young men who had the same desires. We then began to meet at my house on my back deck (we now affectionately call it "deck time"). It was with these eager-to-be-known young men that I posed the deep question about sins. I already knew them all from previous spaces in their lives—most of them I knew due to being their middle school youth pastor, as I was for Alex. Quick side note: this is the beauty of longevity in ministry. I am an old millennial, and as of the writing of this book, I have been at the same church for over eight years. Many older leaders I know assume that millennials don't stay (and don't desire to stay) at jobs long-term, so according to that mind-set, I'm a little bit odd.

With this "life confession," as we called it, these young men went all in. We declared it a safe place, and they chose to be completely open and honest with their confessions. It was an amazing thing to be a part of. The crazy thing was, I thought I knew them but quickly found out that I didn't know them as much as I thought. In the circle, as each man shared his sins, hidden and overt, there was no judgment. I am not aware of a single person who felt judged. It was truly a safe place.[14] Not only was it safe, but these men also experienced genuine love from those to whom they just poured out their life's mess. They grew in their knowing of one another, and I grew in my overall knowing of them as well. This new level of knowing allowed me room to speak into their lives, and I could leverage that through asking even more good, hard questions. Knowing these areas of their lives allowed me to tailor my questions in such a way that we could continue down the road of deeper knowing, as well as into another important relational aspect—growing.

I think it's important here to share some of the best questions I've experienced to solicit the best *knowing* of the young leaders I am grooming for unleashing. Below I give some of the best ones, along with the thought process behind each one. Remember that to get honest answers to these, you must be a safe place. As one who gets to lead and steward young potential leaders, this can be difficult, but it is so vital if you are to get to know them and grow them through questions. As you review these questions, I'm sure some of them will seem like no-brainers. Some may even seem juvenile. I understand that, but have you been asking your leaders these questions? If you have, have you done so while attentively listening to what they're saying and not saying when they answer? Most likely, my guess is you haven't. After each question, I not only give the thought process behind why I choose to ask this question, but also what we should be looking for to know our young leaders better.

Who are the people you most admire and why? The response to this question reveals what specific qualities young leaders see in others and desire to possess and convey personally. The person (or people) they look up to might give you—and them—a picture of who they ultimately want to become. It reveals their desires to themselves and to you, their mentor and leader. This question helps give you a road map of where to lead your young emerging leaders. What should they be unleashed to do? Where should they be unleashed to go? This one question alone can help chart the right course.

What are your biggest fears? A plethora of revelations can appear when you ask this question. First, a response to this question can reveal past pain. Fear of divorce, fear of abuse, fear of loss, fear of insignificance, fear of failure, and fear of abandonment can all take root in some area of past pain. It is essential that we hone in on these types of fears, as it will reveal ways to care for, have patience with, and develop future leaders. Word of caution, however: be careful to *never use their fears against them*. If you receive an honest answer to this question and you manipulate your mentees through using their fears to your advantage, you will lose trust and it will be very difficult to lead them anywhere.

Some of the fears that are exposed with this question are potential areas for growth. A fear of public speaking, for example, could be an area where you consistently and intentionally challenge that person to move ever so slowly out of the comfort zone behind the scenes to take a more up-front role in leadership. After all, part of leadership is leading from the front. This will take time, patience, and generosity on the part of the mentor, who can even direct this process through questions.

What is your vision statement for your life? This question helps you as a mentor developing younger leaders see how young leaders perceive their self and their mission in life. Responses to this question provide a window into whom they are as a person as they succinctly pronounce their purpose. The young leader may be confused by this question and ask what that means. This gives you the opportunity to speak about a "life vision" statement and help them learn how to shape one. You can speak truth into their identity and affirm a strong vision statement. The data shows that the millennial generation and generation Z thrive through words and actions of affirmation—so leverage this for the purpose of affirmation (where you feel you can, of course).

This question, revealing their vision, helps you see how younger leaders view their capabilities. Some personal vision statements are too small and need to be encouraged to be bigger. Other vision statements seem too broad and need help to become more focused and attainable. When we can unlock what people feel their vision is in this life, we can have a much more fruitful relationship, one that leads to deep trust.

Did you ever see your life being where it is now? This question helps uncover the loss of dreams. It also helps gauge satisfaction. Additionally, it could uncover a transformed life. Each of these issues, when uncovered, helps us know our young leaders better. What are some pain points that we can help navigate away from? Do we see any triggers that have affected the loss of dreams? What were the lies these young leaders may have believed about themselves or their capabilities in getting here? All of these issues can be uncovered with this one question—we just need to simply pay close attention in order to know the leader better. Looking from the outside in, many believe those in the millennial generation are narcissists due to the many selfies and self-reflective statuses they post on social media. In some respects, their narcissism is real. I have personally experienced this to be true, and we can use that to our advantage in giving those in the emerging generations space to talk about themselves.[15] When they feel allowed to do so, they feel heard, loved, and appreciated. They will talk about themselves, and this will give us insight into who they really are.

What does your journey to faith look like? With responses to this question, we can see the process (or lack thereof) of discipleship that has occurred in their journey. We will get a glimpse into the depth of their relationship with Christ and can learn where the points of growth or deeper understanding lie in their journey. We can't assume, but we can at least leverage our observations for more detailed questions at a later time. The faith journey of a future church leader is of incredible importance. If we are to trust these young leaders with the future of the church, we better have a real knowledge of their walk with Christ. Many times, this question will also reveal the person's passion or lack of passion for Christ and a specific calling.

Along a similar line of thought, I had a student recently go through an internship for our church's youth ministry. It was clear to me that he was not yet ready to be in full-time ministry, but I wasn't sure how he felt about it. So I asked him to share his "internship journey" with me. It was during his reflection, based on this question, that he concluded he wasn't yet ready. When he finished answering the journey question, he asked me, "I'm not ready, am I?" It offered me an opportunity to speak the truth, but truth infused with encouragement. He had passion; he just didn't yet have everything he needed to sustain effectiveness.

The same type of direction can come out of the journey of faith question, such as the one I suggest. When we add in other questions, such as, "Where do you feel your journey has brought you to now?" we can dig deeper into self-revelatory answers and responses. We will even find that we will experience open doors to answer their questions on these issues honestly. With the beauty of going first, we can also answer the question with raw honesty to give them the freedom to do the same.

There are many more questions that can be asked for the sake of knowing. These are preliminary questions that I have found effective time and again. The key in this type of inquiry process is not interrogation—the agenda should be to simply know the person. When we are asking questions for the sake of knowing, we shouldn't be so quick to jump in with our wisdom, unless, of course, the opportunity arises or an invitation to do so is given. It's simple, really—we are to listen not so we can answer or fix a person, but so we can unassumingly but deeply know that person. If we go into "fixing mode" with millennials and gen Z leaders (or anyone in these generations, for that matter), they will slowly back away, sensing an agenda other than knowing, and we may lose all influence in their lives.

Let's move on to the aspect of asking questions for the purpose of growing the person we are investing in. Many of the questions we previously asked can lead to growing the young leaders while it helps us know them. However, the questions below are set up to walk the young leader down a path toward personal and professional growth. Just like Jesus, we can use questions as a primary means of discipling those we are discipling.

Growing

Many times, to see people grow is to see them mature and come into their own. People really can't grow and mature unless they notice the areas of immaturity and stunted growth. As leaders, we must take the initiative with those we lead to help them see those areas. With the emerging generation, this takes patience and gentleness. Many in the emerging generations are hungry to grow and mature, but (in my personal experience) have found very few leaders who will help guide them with patience and gentleness. The questions below help along this vein of patience and gentleness, drawing those in the emerging generations to a higher maturity and challenging them to see and change the areas of stunted growth.

Asking probing, below-the-surface questions can open doors, letting you impart wisdom, when simply stating the wisdom might fail. If we ask the right question, those in the emerging generations may ask for help answering or may come to the realization that they do not know something they probably should know. This then directs them to you. They will seek your wisdom on the issue, will be willing and hungry, and most likely will even heed your advice or wisdom.

Jewish rabbis (including Jesus) were and are masters of this form of questioning. They can lead a person down a certain path of thinking and direct that person to the answer they want the person to come to without having to answer the questions. A current, well-known author who does this well is Rob Bell. Rob has the uncanny ability to ask the right questions and lead the reader/listener down the path toward discovery and growth. I wrote the following comment about this on my blog shortly after his newest book, *What Is the Bible?* was released.

> Rob's writing is always provocative, controversial and intriguing. He always deals with good, difficult questions and seems to have a good grasp on the questions that are posed about and against the Scripture in our current culture. Rob Bell's approach to the Bible has always been shaped by Jewish theology, especially Liberal Jewish theology and this book deeply resonates with that method, tone, and approach to the Scriptures. He asks questions the way Rabbi's would and unwittingly leads his readers to his conclusions. He writes his conclusions in such a way that they can be read both ways, so he can claim "openness," but if you read closely enough *his true conclusions come out.* Those conclusions are sometimes cryptic, but they are definitely there.[16]

I would say that the main reason many young people find Rob interesting is due to this one fact: *he's asking the right questions.* His provocative, inquisitive style draws people in and gets them thinking, *Yeah, I've been asking that question myself.* Rob engages with many young Christians and non-Christians alike. He sits with them, listens to them, and uncovers what questions they are actually asking. He has discovered the art of knowing in ways many other well-known Christian authors have not. Essentially, his book could be summed up by one probing question. He doesn't ask it in his book, but one can conclude this is the main question being asked. That question is this: *What questions about faith, your purpose, and your future keep you up at night?*

How can we learn the best ways to grow the leaders in our midst? We can seek to uncover where they need to grow by learning the issues that keep them up at night. These issues will reveal some of their fears, doubts, and the overall areas where they are in need of growth. Also, we can uncover many common lifestyle patterns using probing questions with the younger generations. In addition, we can set an environment for our young leaders that is safe, so they can honestly disclose the difficulties and issues that keep them up at night.

As we help those in the emerging generations uncover these areas where there is a need for growth, we can then speak relevant and applicable truth into their lives. There comes a time when questions might cease and we speak directly into present situations, which I'll discuss at the end of this chapter. For now, let's continue to look at more questions that can spark a time of impacting growth.

What areas in your life hinder you from being where you want to be? This question will reveal to both the young leaders and yourself the level of satisfaction that they see in their current position or situation, and the areas they see as pitfalls to the satisfaction they are seeking. This is a self-reflective question that reveals to you, and the young leader, areas in their life that are negatively affecting their ability for growth. The issues that will emerge will be areas you will later be able to directly and succinctly speak into because they've now been revealed and brought out into the open. As with the other questions I strongly encourage you to ask, there is an open opportunity for affirmation. For instance, reply to responses by saying things such as, "Yeah, I can see that too," when they correctly diagnose a blockade to their growth. The younger leaders may even be hung up on issues that really aren't issues, and you can help steer them away from focusing on something that is trivial and help them see the issues that are truly hindrances to their growth.

What lies have you believed about yourself? This is a very intimate and important question. Many times, people are inhibited from growing, due to the lies they believe about themselves, such as the following: you can never measure up, you always mess up, you're worthless, you always have stupid ideas, and the like. We all can be victims to false ideologies about ourselves. These lies about this current younger generation stem not only from families of origin, but also from the data collected about them, which has been used to stifle their voice. For any person, our family of origin has one of the strongest pulls on our identity.[17] When we are told something about ourselves (whether it's true or not), we subconsciously give it power to form our view of who we are. Also, much of the research on millennials in particular (some of which I've cited in the previous chapter and preface) gives cause to many leaders to assume that all people found within that age range act as the research describes.

The great opportunity we have as leaders, in moments of hearing the lies spoken over these young leaders, is to declare them to be untrue. As people of influence in their lives, we have the power (as we are empowered by the Holy Spirit) to break the chain of lies that hold them captive. When you have young leaders who are empowered with the opportunity to shed the chain of lies, they'll come alive. I've seen it true in my life and in many other young leaders I've blessed to unleash. Walking through a course called Personal Spiritual Formation (PSF)[18] in college taught by Dr. Ron Walborn, I was able to establish not only an understanding of lies I've believed, but also ways to invite God to speak the truth of who I am by God's Word and Spirit. One such lie I believed was that I was never good enough. I would strive, but simply couldn't measure up. I became a chronic people pleaser and was stymied many times by decisions because I didn't want to make the wrong choice. I had one student leader believe she was worthless due to repeated abuse from her father, who repeatedly said just that. She believed it to her very core. Yet walking through PSF with her and challenging her to allow God to not only expose the lies she's believed, but also to speak truth into her life, she was set free from these lies. This could very well be their biggest form of growth under your leadership . . . so go after it.

What do you find is true about you that you wish weren't? On the flip side of lies, there are truths about ourselves that we dislike—failures we remain slaves to—and emerging generations are not immune to possessing those nasty truths either. When we can help them uncover these disliked yet very real truths, we can begin to walk with them in the restoration and healing process, as well as move toward transformation in these areas. This can open up a time of honest confession during which they discuss certain sin patterns or unhealthy habits they know they need help to change. Often, we will discover that these issues, which can bring so much frustration, stem out of the fabrications we believe. For example, one of the traps I fall into is that I find myself trying to be a people pleaser, and this has been the case for a long time in my life. The fact that my behavior stems from a fabrication of truth can sometimes make me feel and believe that I'm not good enough. We must ask the Holy Spirit to help reveal these connections, so we can effectively and powerfully work on these issues to become transformed.

I'm sure by now you're thinking to yourself, *I can't just ask questions all the time. At what point do I need to impart my experience and wisdom? I will need to guide, direct, and boldly declare deficiencies I see.* Yes, yes, you will eventually need to do that. There will be times when we must make hard or encouraging assertions. There will be times when we are to impart wisdom and show direction. We must advise, of course, but my main premise is that by knowing these young emerging leaders and by asking the right questions, more often than not, they will invite your wisdom and advice; you won't have to whack them with it out of nowhere. Let me flesh this out from my own life. Earlier in this chapter and in chapter 1, I mentioned Dr. Ron Walborn. He and several other godly men have been supremely influential in my life. Each of the godly men who have spoken into my life began the mentoring process by taking time to know me. These men challenged me with questions, and it was clear they cared more about me as a person than merely as a pastor. They asked difficult, bold questions that were not always easy to answer. One such time was when I was struggling in my first church. I was twenty-two, recently married, about to be a father, and in full-time ministry. I began bumping heads with my senior pastor and was ready to just throw in the towel. I called Ron and a guy named Doug (another mentor of mine) and shared my frustrations with them. I explained my desire to be done, walk away, and find another church. I ranted and raved while they simply sat and listened. When I was done, Doug asked me, "Have you ever read *A Tale of Three Kings*?" I confessed I had not. He told me to go read it, and after I read it, I needed to determine what kind of king I would be and how I would handle the other types of kings in my life. He told me something I didn't want to hear: "Stick it out."

When I brought the issue to Ron, he had very similar advice. He stated, "Stay the course, and learn how you will lead—or not lead—while you are being led under the type of authority and influence you are under now." This was not the advice or the wisdom I wanted to hear, but it was exactly what I needed. Notice, however, I invited their feedback. I brought them into my situation because I knew they were safe: they loved me and *knew* me. They didn't see from afar what I needed and force their opinions on me; I welcomed them into the situation and knew I could trust their advice.

The reason some young leaders are not asking you to give advice or seeking out your wisdom may be that they don't feel loved by you, known by you, or safe with you. Maybe they know you're just going to offer your strong opinion anyway, so they just wait for you to declare what you think is best . . . then they ignore your advice. The key is having a plan to know and grow with the young leaders you are mentoring. When they know that we are for them and not against them, our relationships with the upcoming generations will change.

Finally, I realize I gave a laundry list of questions. I hope you take time to answer those questions for yourself and, when you ask them of your younger leaders, you answer them honestly alongside them as well. Invite them into your life and your past, so they can learn vicariously through your mess. Also, realize that these questions are not exhaustive and that the most important thing is reliance on the Holy Spirit. You may never ask any of these questions, but the Holy Spirit will lay others on your heart. Ask those questions—seek out the guidance of the Holy Spirit. Don't try to wing it when it comes to unleashing the emerging generation. Millennials and gen Z young people don't need just you; they also need the shared guidance of the Holy Spirit. Live as an example.

CHAPTER 3

LIVING ON DISPLAY

Focus on working on your own development and on what you teach. If you do this, you will save yourself and those who hear you. (1 Timothy 4:16)

More is caught than taught.
—Various

If your actions inspire others to dream more, do more and become more, you are a leader.
—John Quincy Adams

WHEN I WAS IN COLLEGE, I WORKED AT A RESTAURANT. The restaurant's manager made not just a request, but a demand to make sure the entire staff went to a monthly meeting. This leader developed a long list as to why these team meetings were important and made a very pointed statement: "These meetings are not suggestions. They are mandatory, so make sure you do whatever you can to make it to these meetings." The very next meeting, the leader was nowhere to be found. I remember feeling outraged by the hypocrisy. The whole staff complained to the assistant manager about the lead manager's absence. We pressed her to give an answer for the lead manager. When we asked the lead manager why he was absent, he simply said he neglected to do something he should've done earlier. He himself did not make the mandatory meeting a priority, but demanded the staff do so. From the next meeting on, many of the staff ignored the mandatory meeting because of the example set by the lead manager. Out of sheer disgust for the hypocrisy that was displayed, the staff wrote off the "mandatory" mandate and made it optional once again.

Leadership is more than talking. Leadership is more than training others, teaching others, or telling others what to do. Leadership is a life. A leader's life will reflect that person's leadership. It's not just how a leader leads in an office or in business. A leader's life shouts in every aspect the leadership that person contains. Leaders need to reject living in such a way that contradicts what they are asking of those they are leading. As leaders, I'm sure you've heard all the inspiring words on this idea of displaying leadership and not just talking about it. I do not think, however, that many have dug deeper into this issue. How much life do we share? Do we simply display this leadership in our organizations? What other areas of my life are being watched? Why is this seemingly more important to these younger generations? With this chapter, I hope to encourage and enlighten you in these areas.

The first thing leaders need to recognize as it pertains to living on display is this: every aspect of a leader's life is an exhibit—not just life within the organization but life outside the organization as well. This is why Paul exhorted Timothy in 1 Timothy 4:16 to keep watch over himself—not just his job, or his image and actions in front of the church. Paul encouraged Timothy to keep watch over his whole self, his whole life. Paul understood that every aspect of our lives can be leveraged for good or for ill, so we must keep watch over our whole self. Whether we like it or not, as leaders we are on display. The younger leaders in close proximity to leaders are watching everything those leaders do. The young leaders are watching the marriages of the leaders, their home life, and their reactions to organizational and personal pain. The question is: do we as leaders realize the reality of our lives being watched? Do we embrace it or simply ignore it?

Leadership has areas of high pressure. I'm sure many of you reading this right now are feeling more pressure to have every aspect of your life "together," but that's simply not possible, nor is it my point in writing this chapter. If I were to tell you, "Your whole life is on display, so make it perfect," you should (and most likely would) close this book. This concept wouldn't help you with this current generation of young leaders either. Perfection in leadership is a mirage, a false facade that those in the emerging generations are highly capable of dismantling. So, pretending will get leaders of young leaders nowhere. Leaders have to embrace the reality of their lives on display and seek to live honestly in every aspect of their lives. This couples well with the main idea in chapter 1—living without masks.

Not only do the young leaders around an older leader desire to be known by that person, but they desire to know that leader as well. What makes the leader tick? How does the main leader overcome adversity? How does their leader celebrate wins? How do leaders grow from failure? How do leaders deal with pain? How does their leader wrestle with personal struggles and weaknesses? All of these areas are teaching points the emerging generations are seeking to learn from you as a leader. Whether those in the emerging generations know it or not, they are constantly saying of the lives of their leaders: "I hope to be like that" or "I hope to *never* be a leader like that." Take a moment and reflect on the leaders and mentors in your life—whether good ones or bad ones. I'd bet for most of us leaders, their lives, reactions, and interactions in the areas above (and others, most likely) have helped shape who we are as leaders. I know for me, from my personal experience, this is most certainly true.

When it comes to the importance of living a leadership life, what do we as leaders do to help leverage our lives? How can leaders allow themselves to be better known by these young leaders? How can leaders open up a deeper trust and know these young leaders as a result? I will take the rest of the chapter to lay out powerful ways we can answer all of these questions. I think the first task is to live with honesty.

Live with Honesty

I think the most powerful form of leadership is being honest and transparent about shortcomings and weaknesses. When leaders make a bad decision, they should own it. When leaders are struggling, they should be absolutely honest about it. One of my mentors, who was overwhelmed by deaths, family addiction issues, and taking care of his grandkids, tried for a time to simply toughen up and push through life and ministry. Once he realized he couldn't, he had to admit that he was tired and needed help. Everyone knew the leader was tired and was struggling, but no one encouraged him to declare it. Shortly after the leader realized he couldn't muscle through it, he openly told the staff, "I'm tired. I need your help." The issues going on were family issues. It wasn't organizational, but it was clear he was being depleted and not recharged enough to keep up the same pace.

His honesty inspired me. His honesty allowed him to have more time and space to deal with the issues that were bogging him down, but it also opened lines of trust with his staff so that we could fill in the gaps he needed us to fill. He opened his life and let his staff in. We don't need to open up about every single issue in our lives because we'd overwhelm those we are leading. However, we must live honestly, especially when we know a specific area is being watched and people are dialed into where we are at with that area. This takes honest evaluation. My mentor took time to look at how his life issues were affecting his work life and leadership capability. He saw he could trust his team, so he released things that were overloading him. We must do the same. This helps the young leaders see that we aren't tone-deaf to our issues and that we are willing to be honest. You will see that this idea stems from and expands upon the ideas presented in chapter 1. They all flow together. Living honestly will lead to the next way that leaders can gain trust with the emerging generations: confessing when they've messed up.

Confess Your Mess

As leaders, our messes are a bit more public (whether private or corporate) than the average person. When leaders mess up, they can shift blame, pretend it never happened, or offer confession. In my experience, there's one overarching and appealing model for the younger generations of leaders—offering confession. Too often we see leaders ignoring their mess-ups. One small, very public example of this is when President Trump recently rejected the notion that he made a simple mistake in spelling on Twitter. The spelling error was pointed out to President Trump, but he attempted to pretend it was something he did purposefully rather than simply admitting he made an error. Many people criticized Trump, but this is the story of many leaders, not just him. The worrisome point for me is, if leaders are unwilling to confess a mess in such a small matter, how much more unwilling are they to confess with bigger issues?

I've seen time and time again respect grow for my leadership with my young leaders when I confessed an issue. When I recognize my failure and confess it publicly to them, they do not lose respect for me. I remember sitting with some of my younger leaders and confessing my deep-seated issue of entitlement. I had expected to be involved in something going on in the larger church body, but it happened without any of my input. I felt cheated and soon recognized my arrogance. The younger leaders and I were discussing pride, and I felt compelled to share my sin of pride showing its ugly head in my attitude and behavior of entitlement. This confession, in turn, brought deep respect for my honesty rather than rejection. My mess of entitlement was also hindering my ability to minister well to them, so I took time to confess that as well and to apologize for my sin hindering my leadership. I don't always do this nor do I always do it well; however, every time I do confess, it helps my leadership. It doesn't hinder it.

The lie that leaders hear and believe is that they will lose respect if they are honest about their failures. I have found, however, that this lie is not true—in most cases—with emerging generations. Belief in this lie is hindering the ability of many leaders from unleashing the leaders of tomorrow. Leaders do not have to be perfect. Leaders do not have to have it all together. Leaders do not have to "prove" they deserve to lead by acting perfect. Leaders lead. Therefore, leaders must come to grips with this: they will mess up and people will see their mistakes. When leaders mess up, it's not going to be quiet. In fact, it may be the buzz of their organization. Leaders can ignore their failures and mess-ups, excuse them away, or own them. When leaders own those failures, shortcomings, and mess-ups, their young leaders see that the leader is serious about honesty and, I believe, will respect them more for it.

Apologize

Confession is one thing. Apologizing is another. When leaders mess up, especially when they sin against another, they must be bold and apologize, ask for forgiveness, and seek to no longer sin against that person. Apologizing models humility, and if leaders are to lead as Jesus led, they must learn humility. When one observes the life of Jesus in the Gospels, we can see several instances of this humility. The most well-known story of humility is when Jesus washed his disciples' feet in John 13. Another well-known story of the humility of Jesus is when he asks John the Baptist to baptize him. Even John knew he was of lower status than Jesus, yet Jesus humbly undertook being baptized by John. If leaders desire the young leaders they are leading to model humility, those leaders must seek to do it first.

I've had two major situations in my life where a leader has deeply wounded me. One leader apologized for wounding me, and the other did not. When I think back on both leaders in my life, it is difficult to pinpoint many good aspects of the one who neglected to apologize and easy to pinpoint the good in the leader who did apologize. They both wounded me in the same manner, but that unmet need for apology grew deeper wounds within me and caused me to eventually seek to leave the leadership of the leader who failed to apologize. I felt unwanted, invalidated, and juvenile. Due to my own immaturity, I held a bitter grudge against this leader for two years and allowed his sin against me to plague my leadership. God did a work in my heart, and this leader and I were able to reconcile, but I had to initiate the forgiveness to see this happen. When I have sinned against someone, I've seen the value in leadership of making the first step and asking for forgiveness as soon as I can be honest.

This is not something to implement with just staff or young leaders who are being raised up either. Leaders should be quick to apologize in their families, with their kids, and with their spouse. Whether leaders notice it or not, these things are seen. When leaders can keep short accounts with everyone in their lives, it is felt and proves the sincerity of their leadership in every aspect of their lives. This assists in keeping watch over oneself, as Paul urged Timothy to do in 1 Timothy 4. Living honestly, confessing, and apologizing are great ways to live on display. Being teachable is another. More is caught than taught, so if a leader is to expect teachability in those under him, he, too, should display his own teachability.

Remain Teachable

As much as we'd like to think we do, you and I do not know everything. Many of my failures have come as a result of forgetting this simple truth. I've struggled with pride a lot in my life, and so I feel as if I must put on a front of "all-knowing" in my areas of expertise. God began breaking me in this area of my life when I began to lead young leaders at our college church. When I began the college church, which we named Aletheia—in Greek it means "unconcealed truth"—I felt I needed to prove to my young leaders that I knew more about church, the Bible, Jesus, and leadership than they did. I was young and felt I needed to prove myself to my leaders as well by displaying a competency birthed out of vast knowledge. All of this proved detrimental to my leadership. The point of naming the church Aletheia was to express our desire and practice of open, honest, authentic, and unhidden church, bucking the trends of the current fake church culture. Yet in my youth, I found myself pretending anyway.

The leaders overseeing me saw me as the arrogant person I was from time to time (when I couldn't hide it well). The younger leaders, whom I was seeking to grow and train, saw me as an unteachable person who was unwilling to hear their advice or ideas. God used many wise people to speak into my life the power of teachability. One mentor suggested that I take my most prized area of "knowledge" (my preaching and sermon prep) and submit it to my student leaders for critique. I cringed. No way would I want to send my student leaders my manuscript before I preached it. What if they changed it and I didn't like the change?

After some bristling, I went with it and saw that many times, my students added good thoughts, helped with application, and helped me craft a more impactful message to the college demographic. My leaders felt investment in the church service like never before, and they saw that I was willing to be teachable. I admit it was very difficult in the beginning and remains a difficult task to submit my sermon manuscript to critique, but I know it makes me and my sermons better.

As leaders, we must also remain teachable in our willingness to learn through seminars, books, and other areas of education. When our young leaders see that we continue to push ourselves to grow, to learn, and to adapt with new knowledge, they then seek the same for themselves. If leaders simply recycle all the same old same old models and such, the younger leaders will notice. Our leadership with this generation will slip if we aren't consistently seeking to grow ourselves. The old adage, "Readers are leaders, and leaders are readers," is remarkably true. We live in a changing world that rapidly moves away from what it once was. Leaders must remain cognizant of that change and remain willing to learn, adapt, and grow within in it. A hunger to learn is an admittance of the need for more knowledge. As leaders, it would behoove us to also set up places and spaces for our young leaders to learn from others besides ourselves. Young leaders may need help with funds to travel to conferences and trainings and to purchase books; leaders can benefit from meeting these needs. Unleashing young leaders is not just spreading a leader's legacy. It's about maintaining the future of the organizations. Leaders must seek to invest as much as they can in the people they are grooming to be the future leaders of their organizations. When leaders model teachability, it will be an aspect of their leadership that will be caught.

Leverage Life Lessons

When leaders impart wisdom, I've found this generation is most receptive to personal life lessons. I'm sure you've noticed this by now—I use my life stories to teach. This is not because I'm all about myself. This is not because I think my life is the only example there is. This is not because I want people to look at me and think I've got it all together. I teach with life stories because they are the most relatable stories. They are the easiest tools in my toolbox, so to speak. I also use personal stories and life lessons because it allows me to be known by my audience. I try to let everyone I teach know I am a real, live person. Sometimes as leaders of leaders, we can become larger than life and so seem to have unattainable leadership results. Many leaders may revel in this sense of importance, to their detriment.

When leaders tell real-life stories, they display the reality that God can use them, with all their wrinkles and warts. In my opinion, young leaders need to see this. Also, to be clear when I say to use life stories, leaders have to share their failures as well as the successes in their stories—the areas where the leaders got it right *and* the areas they learned from when they got it wrong. When leaders get to know those in the emerging generation and then see a similar story unfolding in a younger leader's life, that older leader can leverage their life story. When leaders desire to teach those in the emerging generation a truth about leadership, they can use a story of a moment of failed leadership they experienced to teach it.

Jesus taught with stories. Granted, they were not parables about himself per se, but he leveraged stories to teach. Leaders must do the same. If leaders desire to be known by the people they are leading, they must share personal stories.

Invite In

Before I go into the idea of inviting in, I want to share that boundaries are important. I don't want you to think as you read this segment that I am in any way suggesting that we chuck out boundaries and are always with people. I do believe, however, that leaders must invite the young leaders they are raising up into other areas of their lives and not just the organizational segments of the leader's life.

Inviting in is the concept of bringing these young folks into your home and letting them see your life at home with your family. Give them a window into how you lead there, but also how you keep all the balls in the air when it comes to your life. Simply start by asking yourself these few questions to see if you are doing this:

Have I been inviting the young leaders I'm developing over for dinner with my family?

Have I invited one or all of them into a hobby of mine?

Have I brought them along in my times of seeking direction from the Lord?

Do they know my spouse and kids?

The answers to those few questions will reveal whether you've been inviting in or not. The reality is, in our current culture the younger leaders you are training may not have seen a healthy family life. They may have never been invested in as a person outside of what they could produce. They may have never known what a good balance of ministry (or any other organizational leadership) and family life looks like. They need to know about all areas of life and learn from your life as an example.

There are a number of young couples my wife and I spend time with and pour into. One particular couple feels called to ministry overseas. They are energetic, Spirit-led and deeply loving people. They asked if we could come alongside them and help them understand marriage and ministry. We rejoiced at the opportunity. However, we don't meet them at a restaurant or coffee shop. We bring them into our home. They know our kids. They see our messy living room. They experience the hectic nature of family life. We talk to them about marriage, family, and ministry all before we open our mouths. I have found this has been one of the most powerful things my wife and I have done in the lives of young leaders.

My wife and I didn't set out thinking this way, but have learned it along the way. Now, seeing its power, we invite folks over to our house often.

Young leaders, especially in the millennial and gen Z generations, can benefit from being invited in. Those in the emerging generations can also benefit from a better picture of leadership than the normal nine-to-five office time. Those young leaders can know you, and when they know you, they can trust you. When they see parts of our lives are simply not all neat and tidy, they begin to recognize those who lead them are not some Greek gods with unattainable leadership skills. They see their leader is just like them.

Lastly, when leaders invite into their lives the younger people they are taking time to grow, the younger people will begin to invite those leaders into theirs. Leaders of these younger leaders will get to see a better picture of what makes the young leaders tick, not just what they produce at work. Leaders may see areas where they can encourage their younger leaders and tell them they're on the right track. Leaders may also see some cracks that they themselves may have had and can help guide the younger leader to victory in those areas. This opens up a whole new level of growing, training, and unleashing. Leaders are making great strides toward unleashing well-rounded, healthy leaders when they get involved in more than just their working leadership skills. This is the power of knowing. When leaders know their young leaders, those young leaders feel loved, heard, and encouraged. When those emerging leaders know us, they begin to see that they can trust their older leaders. When young leaders trust their leaders, those trusted older leaders will have great influence in shaping who the younger leaders are . . . and the younger leaders will listen because they *know* it is coming out of a place of love and passion for them.

CHAPTER 4

DREAMS, VOICES, AND FAILURES

Hold fast to dreams, for if dreams die life is a broken-winged bird,
that cannot fly.
—Langston Hughes

THINK BACK TO THE TIME WHEN YOU WERE A YOUNG, naïve, and impressionable child. The biggest question that you most likely received from adults was, "What do you want to be when you grow up?" That was a question about your dreams. I don't know what you said, but I remember saying all kinds of outlandish things: I was going to be a doctor, a professional athlete, a pastor like my daddy—just to name a few. When these dreams were exposed, they were either nurtured or negated. The dreams we are willing to share also give a window into who we are and are an important part of our being known. When we hear the dreams of others, we are getting to know them as well. When we were young, the adults in our lives had the ability to help shape our dreams, for good or for ill. Leaders also have the same ability; they, too, can nurture dreams or negate them.

Let me share with you two examples, one bad and the other good. An older man known by my friend had a dream negated. When this man was young, he was the athlete of all athletes. Since the day he could walk, his father had him playing sports. His dad would get him involved in every sport imaginable. He'd be in baseball, basketball, hockey, and football. His dad pushed him to be the best, urged him to push forward and to never give up on the dream of sports. The only problem was, even though he was decent at sports, it was the dad's dream, not the son's dream. The man's personal dream was to be an artist. He felt alive when he was creating, not when he was tackling, dribbling, skating, and so forth. When he was younger, he told his dad his dream of being an artist. His dad's response was, "That's for girls. You're a man. Don't waste your life trying to be something as dumb and insignificant as that."

With those words, the father of this aspiring artist crushed the little boy's dreams. He knew if he pursued anything other than what his dad thought he should pursue, his father would look down on him and possibly reject him. So, he silenced the longing for this dream to be an artist. Eventually, he became a lawyer. Being a lawyer was respectable. Being a lawyer made him wealthy, powerful, and important—all things his father pushed him to believe were the most important attributes of a man. Yet this son could never find contentment. He kept pressing through, but he wasn't passionate about who he was or what he was doing. He lost the sense of wonder and the desire to dream.

One day, however, God broke the man when another person asked what his dream was as a kid. He went back to his passion for creating. The Lord reminded him of how passionate he was about art. When he shared that his childhood dream was to be an artist to the person who asked about his childhood dream, God used the other person to speak the truth into his heart and life: "You were created to be an artist . . . now go be one!" The freedom that God released to him that day to be what he felt he was created to do was one of the most powerful things this man had ever experienced in his long life. The transformation was remarkable. He began to do art again and even had the chance to sell some of his work. God reignited a dream, and this man was changed. Dreams are vital to who we are and what we do.

The other story is a slightly better story, and it is continuing because it involves my son. Knowing the power a father has over the dreams of their children, I determined to be a dream-encouraging father. My son, who is now eight years old, lives with tons of dreams. Recently, he came up to me and said, "Daddy, I want to be a pro football player for the Pittsburgh Steelers. I want to be their running back." As I heard this, I was immediately tempted to do what the other father had done. This was a ridiculously difficult dream to see come to fruition. How can I encourage my son's dreams of pro football? I will confess, I prayed for guidance because I refused to squelch his spirit. Here's what I said: "Well, buddy, that's a pretty big goal. In order to get there, you'll need to invest a lot of time in training. We'll have to get you in as many football camps and on as many teams as we can. It's not going to be easy, though, bud." He then happily walked away. I'm sure there are a thousand stories of how I messed up his dreams, but this was an example of how God used me to lovingly encourage, but realistically help his dreaming.

Emerging generations need to be allowed to dream. Two chapters ago, I brought about several questions we should be asking the young leaders that we lead. I purposefully neglected to dig into an important question: "What are your dreams?" When leaders ask this question, we need to allow them space to be honest. Those in the emerging generation must know their leaders and mentors are not going to laugh or shoot down their dreams. It must be safe. When the younger leaders feel safe to share their dreams, feel encouraged in their dreams, and are even offered help to attain their dreams, they will ignite with a passion and power like you've not seen before from the young leaders around you. They will feel cared for, empowered, and released to pursue after that which they've been dreaming about. You as a leader can help nurture or negate these young leaders by how you discuss and release their dreams.

In my own life, when I was a much younger leader, I was asked to dream. I was given license to dream big and dream into my future and some future possibilities. I excitedly, and maybe with a bit of naiveté, shared this big dream of mine. The dream I had was to make our organization one that became an education center for urban others. Our organization could pass on to the next generation some of the things we had learned. I had planned out a year of classes and placed people I am close to as the teachers in this model. I also developed an idea for internships. The folks I presented it to were excited by my dream and encouraged me as I shared it. They were automatically thinking of ways they could empower and enact the dream. This was great. I felt charged, loved, and cared for. This elation didn't last long, however. Once the main leader of this project heard what I had presented as my dream, he was angry with me. He felt usurped in some way and vehemently shot down my dream in this area. I remember being deeply wounded, offended, and frustrated. I was asked to dream, was encouraged in my dream, and then crushed. It extinguished my spirit for a time. I lost vision for this dream because it seemed to only bring pain.

I realized then the power and influence of a leader to speak into the lives of those they lead. I didn't know it until then, but I know it now. I also know that in this area of dreams, I am not alone. Millennials and gen Z young leaders alike feel this way about their dreams as well. Here lies a large disconnect from previous generations. Those in the boomer generation (and gen X to some degree) were constantly told to fall in line and not dream. The leader is the leader. Don't imagine a different path and don't think visionary thoughts because that's the main leader's job. When a boomer or gen X leader brings this attitude to the table with young millennial or gen Z leaders, they (the young leaders) shut down. They may still do the work they are tasked with, but they feel undervalued, uncared for, and to some degree unsafe. They have vision, passion, and a view of what the future could be. We, as the leaders who are grooming them for leadership, must give room for them to dream.

Maybe you're thinking, *What if their dream is impractical? How do I approach that situation?* Some dreams will absolutely be impractical and unable to fully be pursued. This is where we lovingly guide through the power of questions. We can ask tough but pointed questions such as the ones below:

How would the implementation of that dream look?

Would this be practical in this context or would the context of the dream need to be changed?

Is it time for this dream or would there be a more suitable time?

The key with these questions is that they do not shoot down the dreams of emerging leaders. The questions are designed to empower the young leader to think about how this dream could (or couldn't) work. This is key. Lastly, as it pertains to the dreams of these young leaders, it's important that we, leaders who are seeking to unleash younger leaders, seek to help them reach their dreams. I'm aware that this may not always be possible, but if it is, leaders should do their best to help the dream come to fruition. I'm not saying we help the younger leaders fulfill their dream to completion, but we can help them get on the right path.

I'm blessed to have a mentor in my life who gets this. As I write this, I am the pastor on staff at a large church in the inner city of Pittsburgh, but I was sent out to the University of Pittsburgh to plant a college church on campus. I've been working with college students and young adults for over six years. As I'm growing and changing, I've been feeling a desire to lead a church that is not comprised of mainly college students and young adults. I've shared this with my lead pastor (Rock Dillaman), and he asked, "How can I help you get there?" He saw my dream, my potential, and is now mentoring me to be unleashed in this dream. I meet with him weekly and simply ask him questions that he takes time to answer. I've never felt more invested in with a dream than I do right now.

So, what I'm saying when I say, "Leaders should help their emerging leaders get on the right path," is that if it is in our power to guide them in getting to their dream, as Rock did with me, we should. Even if it means that unleashing these emerging leaders means releasing them to a different church or a different organization, leaders should empower them to go after their dreams. (I will go more in depth with this in the section on releasing.) As I said before, when we do this, we will be igniting a passion within those in the emerging generations. This dreaming also means that leaders are releasing them to have a voice. A person can't share a dream without speaking it out. A dream is something that is developed within, and in order for others to hear and envision the dream, the dreamer must speak it aloud.

The young leaders in our midst desire to be heard. They desire to have a voice. They feel a strong urge to have a seat at the table, where their voice means something. Sadly, as I look around at many older leaders, the younger leaders in their ranks aren't heard and many times aren't even offered a chance to speak. Like the importance of dreams, having a voice allows these young leaders to feel and be valued by the organizations you lead. Giving young leaders a voice also gives older leaders a window into the young leaders themselves. When leaders give them a voice, we hear their hearts. We can see what these emerging leaders are passionate about. We can hear what they value. We can also get a picture of how a young leader will lead in the future.

Is this young leader aggressive?

Is this young leader patient?

Is this young leader willing to be wrong?

Is this young leader willing to adjust when there is pushback on that person's thoughts or visions?

We could ask the leaders in the emerging generations these questions about themselves, but they may not be able to honestly answer until those situations arise. Giving a voice to the young leaders also gives the others you are leading a new respect for the young leaders. The others you may be leading will get to know these young leaders, and the young leaders will begin to have authority in the organization. This opportunity for voicing their ideas also makes them feel empowered. When young leaders feel empowered, whether by sharing their dreams or by having an opportunity to have a voice in the organization, they will be all in or at least more invested in the organization than they were before.

As leaders who desire to hand the future over to the emerging generations, we must hear their voice and seek to implement some of what they bring to the table. Leaders can't allow the young leaders close to them to voice their ideas and never do anything with the ideas presented. This has the same effect as shooting down a dream. The younger leaders will begin to shut down and will ultimately be less invested in the organization you lead. They will stop sharing their ideas or opinions, and our organizations will suffer from their silence.

When I have this conversation with older leaders, many times they respond with something along the lines of: "This sounds like just another example of how we must coddle the millennials. It sounds like we need to stroke their ego. They are always seeking validation. They need to earn their place at the table by proving themselves." My response is twofold. First, I concede that in my experience, millennials and gen Z young people are more sensitive (at least outwardly) than previous generations when it comes to being heard. This stems from several different areas of their childhood/upbringing (which can't be unpacked in this book). Second, I ask the older leaders to go back to when they had to "earn" their way, and I ask them how that felt. Many times they will respond to this question by stating that they wished it was a little bit different. They will say they sucked it up because they had to, and so this generation should too. Quickly, however, they see that they have the power to shift this, and they see the value in empowering younger leaders in ways they themselves never were. Truthfully, I believe the folks in the younger generations are simply more willing to express their pain and annoyance than the generations before them. To boomers, this sounds like whining, but if those leaders are honest, they felt inwardly what most young folks today are willing to express outwardly.

Also, when it comes to giving voice to the young leaders in our midst, don't ask their opinion if you already know what you're going to do no matter what they say. This will cause your young leaders to shut down and maybe even declare that you don't care what they have to say. I've experienced this, and it's just not edifying or encouraging.

I was in a meeting in which those present were asked to assess how a particular event went. When asked to assess, we were given license to speak into things that went wrong or could be changed. When it came time to sharing our opinions, every critique was met with defensiveness and every suggestion was ignored. Those asking for the feedback already knew what they wanted to hear and what they wanted to do, so there was no point in giving a voice to the younger leaders. This frustrated the younger leaders and caused them to shut down and get angry. It was set up so that these young leaders (including myself) could've felt empowered, but it had the opposite effect.

Again, I know many boomers, and maybe Xers to some degree, reading this may feel as if this is one more example of "coddling" or "stroking the ego of young leaders," but it's not. Stroking the ego of the emerging generation would look more like telling them they'll never fail, that they're the best, and that everything is about them. Not everything needs to be praised. Not every good thing those in the emerging generations do needs to be lauded, nor do they have to have a word in everything. Giving those in the emerging generations a voice in some things does not mean we are feeding into narcissism. It means we are telling them they have good ideas and their voice matters at the table. As leaders, we don't have to implement everything the young leaders suggest. We don't have to listen to the younger leaders' critiques on everything. We do, however, need to find those nuggets that they bring to the table that are worth implementing and then *implement them.*

Also, as leaders who are leading young leaders and seeking to unleash them, we must not take credit from them when we do implement their voiced action plan or critique. I will discuss this more in depth in chapter 10, "Giving Influence," but for now just understand the idea that when a young leader (or anyone) in your organization has a good idea or critique that will be implemented, credit must be given. This allows others in the organization to see this young leader with a newfound respect. Youth in leadership can be and ought to be done.

As a leader who leads young leaders and is preparing many of them to be unleashed, I recognize the difficulty of this. Every time I have a meeting with my students, I ask the following questions:

What can we do better?

What needs to change?

What are your thoughts on new things we should do?

I always get answers. There is one young leader who always has an opinion, thoughts, and advice. At first, it wore me down. Do we ever do anything right in her eyes? However, as I got to know the heart of this leader, I saw that she really cares about what we're doing. She found Christ at our church and wants others to find Christ too. She's so passionate that she is always thinking of ways to make things better, so when I give her a voice, she brings a list. Not everything that's proposed by her (or the others) can be implemented or changed, but what can be implemented, we do. I also give the leadership team the voice to choose yes or no. I do not arrest full control. I believe in collaborative leadership, and so I release my control in these types of matters. This time of giving these young leaders a voice helps me to see their hearts, as I mentioned with the one young leader. I can see what they're passionate about. I can quickly find their pet peeves. Most of all, I can see their true excitement for the work we are doing.

Once a leader allows dreams to be spoken and voices to be heard, the leader must also allow room for failure. To know someone deeply is to know that person in both success and failure. Each area will give insight into how the young leader reacts when success or failure occurs and thus reveals the person more fully. Failure in leadership can be detrimental, and so many leaders avoid it at all costs. The older a leader gets, the more cautious the person may become. This is in part due to wisdom, but fear also plays a large role in it. Therefore, younger leadership needs to be given a voice; they may propose something so audacious and so grand that it freaks out the older leaders. This will push an organization, but it will also grow them—success or not. The older leaders I know well don't allow a voice to younger leaders because they fear the young leader will fail. Those same leaders don't want the failure of a younger leader to bite them and their leadership in the butt, so they avoid handing things over to the emerging generation.

If leaders are truly seeking to unleash the emerging generation of leaders, they must give them room to fail and let them know it's OK if they fail. We all need to experience failure, especially if we are to lead well. The emerging generation of leaders will be weak in the future if they are not taught how to fail, and this education only comes by failing.

When I was tasked with planting a college church, I was petrified. No one but my wife knew this, but I was not as confident as I pretended to be. Again, I found myself wearing a mask of confidence when I didn't actually have the confidence. I knew God had called me and that was all that was keeping me together. I was petrified because I had no clue how to plant a church, and I hate failing. Everything I had done up to that point had been pretty successful. I hadn't really failed at anything. The potential for failure was high. I was also worried I would ruin my new chance at being unleashed by the leadership at the church. If I failed, would I be fired? If I was fired, would I ever have a chance at leading something ever again?

As my doubts and fears of failure in this campus plant swirled through my mind, I felt compelled to bring them to my supervising pastor at the time—John Stanko. I shared my fears with John, and he said a very simple phrase that set me free: "So what if it fails. You'd learn something, I'd learn something, and we'd all grow. Stop sweating it." John is a leader of leaders. He writes books on leadership and teaches master's level courses on leadership, so if he says, "So what if it fails," I'm OK. I felt freedom to go out and do what I was called to, no longer strapped to fear but unleashed to conquer what I knew I was supposed to do. Leaders help grow those under them better when they leave space for failure.

When it comes to failure, leaders best serve young leaders if they are there alongside when failure does come because it will come. We can't simply give young leaders freedom to fail and then when failure happens, abandon them. Young leaders need to know their leaders have their backs. Young emerging leaders need to feel safe under the leadership of the one leading and guiding them. When something an emerging leader put forth stalls out, their leaders have the opportunity to ask good questions as to what happened. Leaders can also find ways to encourage the young leader in the failure. The two worst things—in my mind, anyway—that leaders can do in situations of failure is (1) abandon the emerging leader and (2) beat up the emerging leader, so to speak, about it. Trust me, those in the emerging generations are hard on themselves in areas they expect to excel in, and they are already beating themselves up about the failure. Their leader does not need to pile on to the pain they already feel. As leaders, we must come alongside them and care for them in the failure. The emerging generations need us to help them grow from failure.

Dreams, voices, and failures all boil down to one issue in the leadership of young leaders, and that issue is trust. If leaders do not trust these younger leaders, they will not give them space to dream. Leaders will not give them a voice at the table, and they will not let them fail. John Maxwell, the "leadership guru," as I like to call him, in his book, *Developing the Leaders Around You,* says this: "Once you have identified potential leaders, you need to begin the work of building them into the leaders they can become. To do this, you need a strategy. I use the BEST acronym . . . Believe in them. Encourage them. Share with them. Trust them."[19]

All of what we've been talking about in this chapter must have the best tool involved. Trust, however, is of utmost importance, for as John Maxwell goes on to say, "Leadership can only function on the basis of trust."[20] When young leaders know that the leader above them trusts them, there is little fear of failure. When young leaders know that their leader trusts them, there is no fear in sharing their dreams. When young leaders know that their leader trusts them, they are not afraid to speak up . . . even if they know the leader above them won't necessarily agree with or like what they say. This trust in them becomes reciprocal; they will trust their leader as well. In order for these young leaders to be known as I discussed in chapter 1, they must come to a place of deep trust. This is why the idea of not allowing masks in your leadership is so vital. Trust is only built by relationship. Deep trust is built upon the foundation of honest, authentic relationships, and the emerging generations, as I've seen in my personal experience, are craving this type of leadership. Books such as *UnChristian*,[21] *You Lost Me*,[22] and *Good Faith*[23] are filled with statistics and tangible proof that this need is legitimate among the emerging generations. As leaders, let us decide to give them the type of leadership that is built on honesty and authenticity.

Let me end this chapter with a brief illustration of trust. Last year I went on a missions trip to a missions site within my denomination. At this site, the interns were all young adults. They were all dedicated, strong, loving, and passionate young leaders. The site is one of the all-star sites in my denomination. In my love for young leaders and my desire to know them, I hung out with one of the young leaders. I asked how things were going and how he felt he was being challenged. He reminded me that the main site leaders had recently left the site for a yearlong sabbatical. He shared with me that he longed for them to come back. I began asking more questions to see where he was at with this change in leadership and why he longed for the other leaders.

His answer was pretty straightforward. He said, "The lead site leaders led with full trust until that trust was broken. The interim leaders that are here now have no trust until trust is earned." He felt stifled, uncared for, and as if he were a child, instead of being unleashed to be the strong, very adult leader that he was. How we trust sets up how we know. How we know is discovered by the questions we ask. The questions we ask help us discover dreams. This desire to know allows us to then trust our young leaders to have a voice and to fail. Unleashing begins with knowing, knowing leads to trust, and trust leads to our ability to equip.

The Power of Knowing

The above segment on *knowing* was meant to challenge you. It was meant to help you learn something new or be reminded of something old, and implement the power of knowing in your leadership. I work with young leaders every day. These areas have proved vital to my ability to train, grow, challenge, and shape the young leaders around me. Although it is important to know our leaders, it is much more important to know the Lord. If we as Christian leaders seek to impart wisdom, we better be connected to the Spirit, so we can speak truth in love to them. Being led by the Holy Spirit of the Living God is the wisdom we need to follow. But before we can lead well, we must be willing to be led, and it should be the Holy Spirit who is our leader.

Once we know these young leaders, they will be willing to listen to our advice. They will be ready to be equipped by us, and we will find them to be more willing to implement our advice. Starting with the aspect of knowing opens more doors of possibility with younger leaders than we ever could've thought possible. Let's now move into equipping these leaders for the purpose of unleashing them into the leadership that God is calling them into, so that they can be as healthy as possible as they move into those areas of leadership.

Part 2
Equipping and Growing Emerging Leaders for Success

CHAPTER 5

DEVELOPING CHARACTER

But the LORD said to Samuel, "Have no regard for his appearance or stature,
because I haven't selected him. God doesn't look at things like humans do.
Humans see only what is visible to the eyes, but the LORD sees into the heart."
(1 Samuel 16:7)

We set young leaders up for a fall if we encourage them to envision what they can
do before they consider the kind of person they should be.
—Ruth Haley Barton[24]

WHEN I WAS IN COLLEGE STUDYING TO BE A PASTOR, I encountered a difficult test from a hard, challenging professor. A proctor appointed by the professor while he dealt with some family issues administered the test. As I took the test, I knew I was going to get a C or lower. I had no confidence in my knowledge. The test was on small, theological nuances from the Bible. I should've know everything that was on the test, yet I didn't know much of it. I was frustrated with this test more than any other in my college career. As I went to the professor's door to discuss the test, I saw a note from the proctor (who was also in the class) that said, "Wow, Belsterling, that was the easiest test I've ever taken in your class." I was naturally upset. How could he think that test was easy?

The next day, I found out why the proctor said the test was easy. A friend who was not in the class told me that the proctor cheated and invited two of my classmates to cheat with him. The proctor had received the test the night before from the professor. Then, having the test in hand, the proctor decided to open the test so he could find out what questions were on the test. These three men, who were studying to be pastors and were taking a test on the Bible, decided to cheat. When this was revealed to me, I was livid. They had ruined the curve on our test. I had gotten a C—as did many others in the class. All but these three received a C or lower. I was disturbed at their lack of character. How will these men minister in the church with such low regard for the Scriptures and their own integrity? I had to make a choice—tell the professor what I had discovered or remain silent on the issue. In the end, I couldn't allow their deception to hinder my whole class, so I told the professor. The three of them immediately failed the class and had to retake it.

Character is vitally important. It is our compass for what is right and what is wrong. Bad character will always cause strife and division. As leaders look to instill wisdom in and equip younger leaders, they cannot ignore the importance of character. As I saw my professor fail these three men, I saw a good man making a hard call, all for the purpose of equipping these three men with character. I still know these young men from that class today, and they are men of integrity and character because a leader chose to step in and equip them in their character.

In many secular areas of leadership, the idea of good, strong, moral character is quickly becoming less and less important. Yet character was of high importance to God. When one reads the story of King Saul, this idea of the importance of character becomes quickly apparent. Saul's character quickly began to spiral out of control after he lied to Samuel and blamed the people for his issues, as we saw in chapter 1. God takes time to let us know in 1 Samuel 15:11 that he regretted making Saul king. Not because he was incompetent or because he was an awful king—not yet anyway. He regretted making Saul king due to his poor and rapidly declining character. Character matters to God, and it should matter to us as leaders. As leaders, we should strive to assist in developing good character in those we lead, especially in those whom we will one day unleash.

Too often in building young leaders, we tend to take a deep look at what young leaders can do, produce, or develop rather than who they are as a person. Leaders have a tendency to neglect to really examine the hearts of young leaders or make space for them to examine their hearts with us. This is what Ruth Haley Barton meant when she said, "We set young leaders up for a fall if we encourage them to envision what they can do before they consider the kind of person they should be."[25] Leaders may pour into the skills of younger leaders and neglect their inner lives. This does not help develop character. In fact, it can create a blockage to good character. If people are always praised for what they produce and not who they are, they will begin to care less and less about the importance of growing who they are and will continue to focus on what they can do or produce.

In order to equip young leaders well in the area of character, leaders have to know their emerging leaders well. We've already extensively fleshed out the idea of knowing, but I will quickly say this: if you don't know the young leader, you won't know areas of deficiency in character. If you don't know the areas of deficiency, you can't help develop your leader in those areas.

As leaders, when we develop an authentic community, being transparent about our failures, our past, and our own deficiencies, we will see others open up and do the same. This is a simple overview of part 1 of this book, but I can't help but stress the importance of knowing as we seek to equip. What leaders have, that they desire to pass on, will either miss the mark or be rejected when they do not have a true, knowing relationship with these young leaders. So, how can leaders help develop character in the young emerging leaders they find around them? I will walk through several areas where character can be developed and how we as leaders can initiate or leverage those areas. While leaders seek to teach, equip, and instill lessons in the emerging leaders in our midst, let us always keep before us the ideas of Spirit-led grace and truth, as well as speaking the truth in love. With the emerging generations, leading from anger or speaking out of frustration or accusation will *always* shut them down, and they will shut you out. Be honest, but be loving.

Character Is Developed Through Criticism

Earlier in the book, I talked about giving space for dreams. I shared the importance of giving a voice to young leaders and even giving space for them to fail. In these areas, they most likely will encounter criticism. You, their leader, may be the one giving the criticism or it may be from other staff. With the right heart and motive behind it, criticism can be a powerful tool for learning. It is in these moments you can see the cracks in your emerging leaders' character. The data is true when it discusses the narcissistic nature of the emerging generations.[26] The emerging generations do not like to be criticized. They enjoy being right and may be arrogant in their ability to have a voice. Don't let this make you timid to give those in the emerging generations a voice, however. When they receive criticism, see how they respond. Then leverage the beauty of questions. You can help lead them to understanding and self-revelation by asking hard, honest questions.

You can ask a question as simple as this: how did you feel when I (or someone else) criticized your idea or your opinion on a matter? Getting them to share how they felt, rather than jumping right to their reaction, can be a helpful tool in starting the conversation, and it will go a long way to creating an atmosphere of openness. I know, for me, both personally and with my young leaders, it has been helpful.

I remember being in a meeting, sharing an idea and then noticing that my idea was completely ignored. When I asked why my idea was ignored, the leader of this organization simply stated, "It was an awful idea." Wait, what? Needless to say, I was ticked. There was no soft landing for that statement. I immediately reached out to one of my mentors and began to explain the situation. He listened and asked, "Why did you get so mad when he said it was an awful idea?" I said, "There was no grace. It was so pointed and seemed spiteful." He then asked, "OK, that may be, but what was underneath your visceral response?" I was forced to think hard. The answer was simple: "I thought my idea was best and felt entitled to being heard." Just like that, I could see my real issue—entitlement. I would've sworn I was different from most millennials, but rapidly, my heart and issues were exposed. His honest, gentle probing not only allowed me room for complaint, but also helped lead me down the path of self-revelation.

When leaders see their young leaders bristle under criticism, the leader shouldn't ignore it. The leader must deal with it. Those moments are great times to help develop character in the young leaders. The moment I just shared has caused me to check myself time and time again. My mentor was used by God to help develop in me a stronger character, and he didn't do it through lecture, but rather humble inquiry. Equipping these emerging generations can no longer be done through a lecture-only style. My mentor could've dragged me in the mud and told me I was acting entitled, but I *know* it would've caused more pain for me, and rather than being a teachable moment, it would have had the opposite effect in my life.

In this, I know I am not teaching anything new or earth-shattering. You're most likely a seasoned leader. You have read leadership books that have encouraged you to do many of the things I am discussing in this book. However, putting into practice what we know doesn't always occur. It's key for leaders to take time to leverage those moments of a frustrated young leader for the purpose of character building. Leaders of those in the emerging generations should shy away from the attitude of "put emerging leaders in their place." In talking with many boomers, when they encounter this sense of entitlement, it rubs them the wrong way and they fail to instill a deeper sense of character into their emerging leaders because they allow their own frustration to boil over. After all, many boomers had to wait until their voice was important. Many fought tooth and nail to get to where they are. Why can't the younger generations wait their turn or accept the leader's criticism as a moment of growth in and of itself?

The answer is simple: those within emerging generations are different from you. Their environment is different than the one you experienced. They were told different things about themselves than you were. The truth is, too, that you deserved chances at a younger age that you were denied. When we as leaders (or even as people) bristle against the entitlement of those in this generation, are we responding out of our past pain? Are we trying to make the younger leaders feel what we felt? In my personal experience, I find the answer to be yes, more often than I care to admit.

Criticism is important. Leaders can't coddle the emerging generations, but neither should they do the exact opposite and tear them apart without grace or love. Leaders can't avoid criticizing ideas, visions, or even dreams, but this criticism must be done gently and in love. This is why knowing those in the emerging generations and being known by them is so important. Once they know your heart as a leader and know that you are for them and not against them, these emerging leaders will be more moldable and more willing to hear your criticism. Character is developed through criticism. As leaders, let's use it to our advantage, their growth, and not their detriment.

Character Is Developed Through Disappointment and Struggle

In the life of the historical King David of Israel, David's best teachers for developing a stronger character were disappointment and struggle. He had to toil. He lived with a target on his back for several years. Yet God used that time to refine him and instill in him a deeper sense of trust upon the Lord. In the cave, David grew to be the man of God he was always meant to be. God refined David in those times so that he could have the heart God prophetically spoke over him when he called David a man after his own heart. It was the cave that produced this heart.

The same is true in our own lives, and the same is true in the lives of the emerging leaders we are leading. The key is in how we as leaders guide them through these difficult times. One of the tools I use to help my young leaders through disappointment and struggle is what I call a biblical examination of the heart, in which I walk through the beginning of Psalm 23 and share what the godly heart of David looked like, as a model for what a godly heart would look like in them. I then ask my young leaders tough questions to help them see where they are. David suffered more heartache than many have or ever will, so this is a pretty good test to take and be challenged by. Below is the "exam," the description of a godly heart I give, as well as the questions to ask the emerging leaders.

When we look at our own heart, many times we don't want God to examine it because we know what God would uncover. We spend a lot of time trying to "be godly," but know that our heart doesn't show the same view when truly examined. We really don't know what's going on underneath unless we allow God to do the deep work of real examination. We know deep down that we have stuff hidden within our hearts we hope no one finds. *God examines our heart to reveal our brokenness.* Especially in times of struggle and disappointment, our hearts can be revealed. God's goal in examining our hearts is not to say, "Aha! I *knew* this was here." No, it is to show us our deep need for a godly heart like David's. It was David's heart that God chose, not his face. It wasn't the great deeds David could or would do, but his heart. In leadership, the heart is more important than the potential.

What Does a Godly Heart Look Like?

God chose David because of his heart. What was in his heart that was so godly? What did this godly heart even look like? To see this, I believe going to the first four verses of David's most famous psalm will give us insight into understanding what a godly heart looks like.

A Godly Heart Beats with Belief (Psalm 23:1)

The LORD is my shepherd; I shall not want (ESV).

David was chosen for his heart, a heart that sought after God. In those moments alone tending the flock, David sought after God. This psalm welcomes us to see through a window to the heart of David, a heart that fully trusted and believed in God. David's heart was a believing heart. He knew who led him, he knew who watched over him, and he knew that because he knew the Shepherd, he would not want. He wouldn't need to seek out fulfillment anywhere else. He wouldn't need fame and fortune, and he wouldn't need this thing or that thing. His heart fully believed (for most his life) that God was all he needed and his heart, when satisfied with God, would not want for anything. Being satisfied in God is knowing God is enough. David believed this. We see David's strength in this passage, his strength in his belief. His complete and unshakable faith in God. He found his all, his very self, wrapped up into the identity of his Shepherd: God. The boy who was the shepherd of sheep admitted his own inability to lead himself. He confessed his belief and need of a shepherd who satisfied him to the point of having no wants.

A Godly Heart Is Quick to Be Quiet (Psalm 23:2)

He makes me lie down in green pastures. He leads me beside still waters (ESV).

Being quiet is not an American norm. In fact, even going to sleep is hard for many. Seventy million Americans have insomnia, 64 percent of teens say lack of sleep is the cause of their poor school performance, people ages 30 to 40 and women suffer the most, and insomnia is one of the reasons why coffee is such a commodity in the United States.[27] Getting quiet is scary; we don't want still waters or the silence of green pastures. We want busyness, noise, and hustle and bustle. Here we see that David had a quiet heart, a heart that wasn't afraid to be made to lie down or a heart afraid of still waters where communion with God was the only thing on the agenda. He freed himself to spend time with God, desired the deep richness of the silence, and allowed this to restore his very soul. You see, we need the quiet in order to hear God. We need space to slow down and be quiet. David knew how to do this, to shut out all other voices and noises, and focus on lying down in the quiet to hear the voice of his Shepherd. God won't normally be in the fire or the earthquake, but in the still small whisper. Many people claim to not hear God's voice but never get quiet enough to listen. Reggie McNeal in his book, *A Work of Heart,* says, "Great spiritual leaders are great spiritual leaders because they enjoy exceptional communion with God."[28] As spiritual leaders, are we enjoying exceptional time with the Lord?

A Godly Heart Passionately Pursues Holiness (Psalm 23:3)

He restores my soul. He leads me in paths of righteousness for his name's sake (ESV).

David had a solid understanding that only God could restore him and make him righteous. David in other psalms pleads with God to forgive his sins and to blot them out and then to make him righteous once again. Here he shows the priority this has on his life, namely with holiness. David desired to be an upright man. He pours his soul out to the Lord begging for healing, begging to regain lost righteousness because holiness was important to David. Being set apart, being other than, was a high priority to David. His brothers were passed over for king because they did not have such a heart. Their hearts sought glory and honor for their own sake, but David here humbly realized that everything is for God's sake, not his own, even his restoration. *All that is given, all that is restored, is to be used for God, not for the glorification of self.* David's heart was not one that pushed for the limelight so he could be recognized. Not once do we see David purposefully trying to take the spotlight. He danced in his underwear one time, but even that was for the glory of God, to show that David the king was undignified compared to the Lord himself. David sought holiness.

A Godly Heart Wholly Trusts the Lord (Psalm 23:4)

Even though I walk through the valley of the shadow of death, I will fear no evil, for you are with me; your rod and your staff, they comfort me (ESV).

David's trust in God allowed him to live without fear. Here he says he could be walking in utter darkness of death, where living seems the least likely outcome, yet because God is with him, he will fear no evil. It had nothing to do with David himself, but his safety is completely wrapped up in God. We see this again in action against Goliath. This type of trust can only come through experience and intentional relationship building. David Benner says, "Everything that is false about us arises from our belief that our deepest happiness will come from living life our way, not God's way."[29] Our false façades exist because we do not trust the Lord. This trust came from his being quiet in the fields, not sitting on the throne. It was his time alone with God that transformed him, not his seat of power. This is true also for the times of toil and struggle in the life of David. While he was in the cave, hiding from Saul, who sought to kill him, David trusted God. Despite what comes our way, we should do the same. This is what builds character.

Questions for Reflection

Be honest with these questions:

Does your heart reflect David's?

Is God enough? Or when things get hard, will you turn to something or someone else?

Are you believing and trusting even during struggle and disappointment?

Are you purposefully being quiet, expecting to hear from God?

Are you seeking holiness for God's glory or are you seeking things for yourself, for your glory? Do you trust God will do as God says?

When we are equipping these young emerging leaders, it is imperative that leaders instill within them the desire to be character-driven leaders. In his book, *Protégé*, Steve Saccone says, "A character-driven leader is a leader who becomes *a person with something to say.*"[30] I fully agree with this statement. As leaders, we should desire our young leaders to have something to say, not because of education or powerful gifts, but because their life speaks first. The beauty of unleashing the emerging generation of leaders is that knowing, equipping, and releasing all flow together. They are not simply "building blocks," but each is as important as the other. They all flow and meld together. Leaders also understand that they can't build character-driven leaders without first being a character-driven leader. As leaders, we must allow ourselves to be known, so the younger leaders can catch the passion for such leadership without us having to say much.

The idea of disappointment has been wrestled with as it pertains to growing character; struggle and pain also have this capability. An author on leadership development, Reggie McNeal, says this about pain: "The leader who accepts pain as the work of God in the commonplace grows from it rather than being diminished by it."[31] How can a leader help leverage struggle and pain in the lives of their young emerging leaders so they can grow and not diminish? One of the best ways is by being a safe place.[32] (I repeat this phrase throughout the book because it is a vital piece of leadership for the emerging leaders in your midst.) When a young leader is struggling, be a listening ear. Do not try to *fix* that person. Simply be there. As a boss or a leader, this can be tough because there are certain (personal) things your young leader can't necessarily open up about with you. However, the leader still should feel free to open up about the things they can share. If they find themselves in a "dark night of the soul,"[33] as St. John of the Cross calls it, they will need a strong leader to help them walk through it . . . and in the process help them develop deeper character. Another good way to help allow pain to grow a young leader's character is to ask deeper questions about that leader's thought life. After all, the old adage, "Character is what you do when no one is looking," is profoundly true. Many times the things we do in isolation begin in the isolation of our thoughts.

Character Is Developed in Our Thought Life

In college, when I struggled with pornography (as I briefly mentioned in chapter 1), my thought life[34] was a mess. I began to see women as objects and not humans. My character was beginning to slip, as was my thought life. I knew something must be done, so I reached out to a friend to hold me accountable. We didn't just share when we looked at porn. We delved deep into each other's thought life and how we did or didn't allow our eyes to sin that day. We discovered that our character as it came to viewing women began in our minds. I believe that character in every facet begins in our minds.

Many times in leadership, I have found that people generally try to deal with and change their internal mess by themselves. Most often, the behaviors we see younger leaders living into are manifestations of internal realities. When trying to deal with the externals with our young leaders, we can easily miss the point that deep inner issues most likely are going on. This neglect can end up hindering them rather than helping them. As leaders, we should never seek to win the battle for behavior. We should always seek to win the battle for the heart.[35] There are always ramifications for any behavior (good or bad), but if leaders are truly seeking to unleash good, healthy, and strong younger leaders in the future, they can no longer neglect issues of the heart, *especially* in ministry leadership roles.

A youth pastor who graduated from the same college I did lost the battle inside, and it ended up ruining his whole life. He wrestled in secret with an addiction to porn for years. This addiction led to a desire for a bigger high, so he began secretly attending strip clubs. This led to a deeper desire for the next level of sexual satisfaction. He began soliciting sex from prostitutes and eventually was caught. Had he been honest with his thought life in the very beginning, he would've been able to avoid the loss of everything he declared he held dear. He lost his family, his friends, and his ability to be in ministry, all in one fell swoop.

His lead pastor should've been seeking to reach his heart, know his heart, and help direct his heart to a stronger character. Of course, he still could've hidden everything and maybe nothing would've been different, yet our calling as leaders is to seek to reach the heart of the emerging generation of leaders, not just their behaviors. Spiritual leadership truly is a work of heart, as Reggie McNeal, in the title of his book, *A Work of Heart,* would say, and the best way to see the heart is to be honest with the thoughts we have and no longer keep them to ourselves. As we do so on our own with our mentors, we can challenge our younger leaders to do the same.

I'm thankful for a place where I can go to, to share my heart and thoughts. I have a group of men who hold me accountable and let me be honest about my thoughts, no matter how light or how dark they may be. As a leader, are you leading the way in this? Do you have a place with people who help you process your inner dialogue? If not, I highly suggest you do and challenge the younger leaders under your influence to do the same. Seek also to be a place where they can process some of their inner life. When your younger leaders open up these spaces of their inner life, I guarantee they will give you room to help guide them.

Having the ability to be honest, even with our inner thought life, is true community. Leaders need community. Young leaders need community, especially emerging leaders going into spiritual leadership. This statement by Reggie McNeal is so true: "Not until spiritual leaders are willing to move past the Lone Ranger, heroic-leader model of leadership will they foster genuine community and release its power for transforming lives. No one suffers more from the lack of community than spiritual leaders themselves."[36] True community is working together on issues of the heart, not simply surface-level, superficial stuff. God has done more work on my life through people who seek my heart than through people who seek my behavior. After all, this is how God approached us, isn't it? In the garden, God sought out Adam and Eve. God came to find them. When they were found, God didn't pound them into the mud or even mention their initial behavior. God came to win back their hearts. As leaders, if we are to develop character in these young leaders and seek to do so for the purpose of equipping them for their future (and current) roles in leadership, we must follow the example of the Lord in this.

Character has many definitions. Here, in this chapter, I purposefully brought about a different facet to the conversation on character—a facet that focuses on issues of character not regularly dealt with. This chapter also gives practical tools to help older leaders lead their younger leaders into deeper, fuller, and richer character. Using the tools in this chapter will help leaders see incredible change in the lives of the leaders they are seeking to unleash. Once leaders can see their younger leaders have strong and growing characters, they can begin to further equip them by helping the younger leaders develop influence.

CHAPTER 6

DEVELOPING INFLUENCE

If you don't have influence, you will never be able to lead others.
—John Maxwell[37]

True leadership cannot be awarded, appointed, or assigned. It comes only from influence, and that cannot be mandated. It must be earned.
—John Maxwell[38]

SHORTLY AFTER I BECAME THE COLLEGE AND CAMPUS PLANT pastor at Allegheny Center Alliance Church, I was notified about a group of campus chaplains at Pitt that met monthly. The group was called UPAC (University of Pittsburgh Association of Chaplains). I quickly began to attend these meetings, and as the new guy, I felt out of place and looked at with suspicion. Over the next couple of years, I had to prove my longevity and trustworthiness to these longtime campus ministers. I was made a member of the group and then was able to little by little earn trust and a voice within UPAC. My voice in the meetings soon allowed me to prove myself and gain trust.

After close to three years, I found myself voted in as the vice chairman of this group of campus religious leaders. The very next year, I was voted in as chairman. During my time as chairman, two incidents came up that I had to deal with. One was a group seeking access to campus by way of membership in our association, and the other was a campus church that had been on campus and seeking membership for four years. Both issues were highly contentious, but the grace of God gave me and the rest of the executive team the ability to lead these issues out of turmoil and into resolution. I was able to use the trust I'd earned to influence our chaplaincy to come to a place that recognized the danger of the cult group and the health of the other campus church.

This influence didn't come overnight, nor did the trust UPAC had in me that helped give me influence to guide these contentious decisions. Without the time, effort, and trust built over the last several years, I would never have gained any influence. Yet I earned their trust, and they gave me influence, and so I was able to effectively lead in these and other areas.

Influence is a key component to leadership. Many times leaders may see this as a natural ability, rather than one that can be developed. However, I believe it is something that can be developed in young leaders and also given to them in order to set them up for more success. I once had amazing leadership advice from a boss of mine. I now know it's a common idea, but at the time, I was twenty-one and it struck such a cord with me that in that moment I owned it. He said, "Marv, leadership is like a bank account. Money goes in and money goes out. When we have good influence and we are leading well, we see money go into the account. When we make hard choices, difficult changes, and/or ask hard things of those we lead, many times we will see money go out of our account. Also, keep in mind, Marv, money will *always* come out of our account when we mess up in a way that hinders our influence. Always be aware of how much money is in your account, so you don't make a premature withdrawal."

This was my first lesson in developing influence—simply stated, don't spend capital you don't have. Many young leaders I've known do not live into this truth. Some don't even know this idea exists. Young leaders who can visualize changes necessary to steer a church or organization in a different direction end up doing so before they have the influential capital. They need to first learn their calling, then they must earn trust, and finally, they must lead with patience if they are to gain influence. As leaders of those in the emerging generations, the issues of calling, earning trust, and leading with patience are areas we can help develop influence into the lives of our young leaders. I'll break down each area and draw out ways in which leaders can help develop each one.

Learning Calling

Reggie McNeal says of calling: "God shapes the heart of the leader through the call. This call is a divinely orchestrated setting apart of the leader for some special task."[39]

One can see this truth unpacked in the life of King David. You've probably noticed that I love the life of David. His life and the life of his predecessor have much to teach anyone on the ideas of leadership. David was anointed king over Israel at an early age. Samuel told him in front of his whole family that his destiny was to be the king and that God had chosen him to rule. He had a solid understanding of his call from the Lord, but that calling was going to be tested time and time again. Saul, the current king, would begin to loathe David. He would seek his downfall and even desire to murder David. Yet the call on David's life was what brought him through. The Lord would show him glimpses of his anointing when men showed up at the cave he was hiding in to fight with and for him. God gave David favor in many areas, even when he was living outside his call (that is, when he fled to Philistia).

David's call anchored him and gave him the influence he needed because he stayed the course. He didn't gain the full benefits of his call until ten-plus years after his anointing. Certainty of their call is what we are tasked to help cultivate in these young leaders. The called bring with them not just influence, but also divine influence that contains favor and authority. Again, Reggie McNeal speaks to this: "The anointing is the God-part of the leadership equation. *It accounts for the leader's effectiveness that reaches far beyond what the leader alone brings to the table...* The experience of the anointing is truly humbling to the leader, who knows that unless God shows up, the crowd goes away hungry."[40] Many of you reading this, the ones who are certain in your call, know this to be true, but are you as a leader instilling this in the life of your young emerging leaders? Are we as leaders simply speaking to their work or their capabilities or are we helping them sense, know, and be certain in their call?

I've learned, by watching many friends burn out of ministry or other areas of leadership, that leadership is a calling. If you're not called to lead or pastor, you will burn out. Granted, you can burn out even if you are called, but burn-out is much higher in those who are unsure of their calling. When discussing "calling," I am utilizing this working definition: "a strong inner impulse toward a particular course of action especially when accompanied by conviction of divine influence."[41] The focus in this book on calling is the "divine influence," in which one senses the Lord leading to a particular job or ministry.

If you are a leader and you hate your job, that type of passionless living will begin to spill over onto the people you lead. This is why the idea of calling is so vital to the idea of influence. If we are called, we will be passionate about what we're doing. If we can honestly look at our leadership and declare, "I'd rather do nothing else right now in my life than what I'm doing," we will have influence.

This is an important reality that should be developed in young leaders. We must turn again to good, hard questions. I recently had a discussion with a young youth pastor I've mentored in the past. He reached out and said, "My senior pastor just sat me down and asked me a tough question. He asked me, 'Are you passionate about young people or are you here to just get a paycheck?'" This young pastor shared with me how frustrated he was by this question. It came out of nowhere (I don't recommend this type of question out of nowhere), but bugged him enough to seek my input. He asked me what he should do. He's having fights with his wife about not spending enough time with her. He's now getting flack from his senior pastor for not spending enough time with his students, so what is he to do? He was in a tough place, but I couldn't let him off the hook. He and I have had a lot of time building our relationship, and so I asked him, "What's your answer to his question?" He assured me that he was passionate, but rattled off a list of what his weekdays and nights looked like. He quickly realized he did have little time with his wife and not enough time with his students.

I then asked, "Are there things that are hindering your passion or taking time away from your passion for your wife or your ministry?" He was able to answer honestly that yes, there were a few things. This young pastor was allowing time-taking hobbies not connected to his calling to usurp the richness of his calling. As a result of allowing these things to usurp his calling (both to his wife and his ministry), his influence was beginning to wane. He was seemingly less passionate due to a warped schedule that was out of balance, and as a result, his boss was questioning his passion. Many young leaders do not understand the idea of viewing what they decide to spend time doing through the lens of calling. We all need recreational things that we do just for ourselves, but if we selfishly linger in those things to the detriment of our calling, we need to rethink what we are doing in the matrix of what we are called to do.

How do we help young leaders discern their calling? In his book, *My Utmost for His Highest,* E.M. Bounds said this: "The call of God is not just for a select few but for everyone. Whether I hear God's call or not depends on the condition of my ears, and exactly what I hear depends upon my spiritual attitude."[42] To help young leaders discern their calling, we have to help them have a better condition of listening. We must challenge them to listen to:

- their hearts
- their gifts

- their desires
- the Lord

When young leaders can take time to align these four things, they will have a pretty good idea of what their calling is. When they are discerning their call, if it is apparent they need to shift certain things, challenge them to do so. The ultimate goal of assessing calling is that these young leaders will solidify their calling and as a result begin to increase their passion for what they are doing. *Passionate leaders have powerful influence.* Leaders who are certain in their call *will be* passionate leaders. This is why it is critical to help them become certain in their calling; we, their leaders, should earnestly seek for our young leaders to be passionate.

Let me stop and answer some questions you may be asking: "If they're not certain of their call, why are they in this job? As a leader, why would I invest in them or why would I have not let them go yet?" My first answer is simple—we all need to be revived in our calling. We all need those gut-check moments, and since you are invested in *knowing* these young leaders, you will know when the time to reenergize their calling will be. Second, if in your discovery of knowing your young leaders, you get a hint of a different calling on their lives, it is your job to help guide them to it. You as a leader hoping to groom and then unleash young leaders need to help them find their calling, so they can be most influential in the areas of their passion and calling. Leaders can't set the young future leaders up for failure. Here is where we go back to employing good questions that lead them down a track to self-discovery.

When I graduated from Nyack College, my big dream for myself was to be a youth pastor forever and maybe in twenty-five years be the national youth director in my denomination. Those were my aspirations. I lived into it and was proud I wasn't using youth ministry as a "stepping-stone," as it so often is. I was in New York for three-and-a-half years and then moved to Pittsburgh to be an inner-city youth pastor. My dreams were coming true. I was a youth pastor in a megachurch.

Soon, however, I began to feel a tug outside of youth ministry, but shoved it down and ignored it. I wanted to be a "lifer," and so I was sticking to my guns. I noticed that my passion for what I was doing began to wane, and my influence was suffering as a result. I may have continued to languish there if it weren't for several key leaders in my life who challenged me to think outside of youth ministry. They helped me discern a different calling[43] and through knowing me and asking good questions, they helped me to have a self-discovery as I had never had before. I moved out of youth ministry and into planting a church on a college campus. The amazing thing is this: I have never had so much favor and influence in all my life. The church leadership not only made it possible for me to remain on staff with them, but also made it possible for me to live into my calling. What a blessing! This caused an increase in the church budget and a need to search for a new middle school youth pastor, but they suffered those losses so I could live into my calling. I will be forever grateful. Are you willing to sacrifice in this way in order to grow, develop, and challenge your emerging leaders?

This is what I'm saying when it comes to developing influence in your young leaders through calling. Leaders play a vital role in helping young leaders develop influence. In my opinion, their influence is made or broken on the issue of their calling.

Earning Trust

Leaders lead most effectively when relationships are open and strong between them and their followers. How do you have that kind of relationship with your followers? One word: trust.[44]

If no one trusts you, you will not have influence. People may follow you because they have to, but they will be feet-dragging followers. As leaders, you know this and have most likely found amazing ways to develop trust with those who are following you. When it comes to emerging generations, there is a need for developing influence through earning trust. As the data indicates, the younger, emerging leaders come from a generation where things were handed to them in many respects.[45] Many in these generations have difficulty grasping the concept of earning anything, so there must be space for us as leaders to help younger leaders grasp the power of earning trust. "To earn" by very definition means "to take time." In our culture, many people are not willing to put in as much time as they used to. In TV land, we live in a society of five to seven seconds. In any scene, the camera angle will change dozens of times, so most shows and commercials will change the camera angle to keep people engaged.[46] All this is to say that these younger leaders have grown up in an impulsive, fast-paced culture in which it is hard to take time to earn something, even something as important as trust.

As Gene Wilkes insinuates in the quote above, trust is a relational process. In order to lead well, leaders need good relationships with those who follow them. The relationships that are developed over time lead to trust, when leaders can put their full trust in their followers and their followers trust them as leaders. Good leaders purposefully engage in relationships that lead to trust, and good leaders should seek to instill the importance of such relationships in the hearts and minds of their emerging leaders, so they can develop influence through reciprocal relationship. Leaders need to go first to model the importance of deep, rich relationships, so the emerging leaders can trust them. Good leaders should not only display this sense of building relationships solely with their younger leaders; it also should be across their entire organization. When good leaders display this level of relationship building and trust, the younger leaders around them can glean wisdom on how to relationally build trust and in turn gain influence with the people that the younger leaders will be (or are already) leading. What Gene Wilkes says is true: "You are not the leader until the group you are leading says so."[47] When leaders can display this type of trust with those we lead and then encourage the emerging leaders in our midst to follow suit, we will begin to unleash them to gain trust and thus influential capital. We will discuss the idea of *giving* influence in another chapter, but I will simply ask here: are we encouraged when the young leaders around us increase in their influence or are we living in jealousy like Saul?

If the young emerging leaders gaining more influence do not encourage you as a leader, you have to take time to ask why. If we as leaders know our young leaders to be trustworthy and assets to our teams, then there are very few reasons to be discouraged by their influx of influence. The reason for a leader's discouragement might be an issue that lies solely within that leader, and it ought to be dealt with quickly. We have to be leaders who willingly teach and then unleash. So, how do we continue to develop these emerging leaders in influence? As leaders, we all know the desperate need for patience. In order to take the time to earn trust, we have to lead with patience.

Leading with Patience

"Impatience leads to reaction against events instead of waiting for divine direction. Impatience causes leaders to sacrifice insight for effort."[48]

Many young leaders struggle with the idea of patience. This is not just a younger generation issue either. In my experience, impatience is an issue with leaders from all generations. The energy is higher for younger leaders, the disillusionment is lower, and the desire to move is insatiable. These current generations may have a harder time with patience due to the culture around them. Earlier in the book, I discussed how commercials and television shows have a propensity to flash to different camera angles quickly. Yet TV is not the only place creating a lack of delayed gratification. Millennials and gen Z have grown up in a generation of *right now*. Food is cooked faster. Books, videos, and albums are available at the touch of a button. Letters are delivered in seconds. Shopping is done via the internet as well and can be shipped in two days or less if the buyer pays a little more . . . and many do. Boomers, and to some degree gen Xers, didn't have to live with such immediacy when they were younger, but they are, however, the ones who created the culture of immediacy. The very fact that the boomers and Xers created the culture of immediacy speaks to the reality of their own impatience. The previous generations have designed the society we live in and get frustrated with those in the emerging generations they helped create through the culture of immediacy. Instead of frustration, those leaders in the boomer and Xer generations would be better served by teaching the powerful lessons of patience, and it begins with the patience of the leaders themselves with the emerging leaders they seek to equip.

I remember my dad always said to me growing up, "Son, you need to learn delayed gratification. Good things come to those who wait." I railed against this thinking for a long time, but have come to find out that patience truly is key. Patience develops a deeper maturity that can *only* be developed through waiting. This can be seen in the life of King David. Those days in the cave hiding from Saul were where God was developing a hard-earned patience that helped make David a great leader. David didn't try to usurp Saul. He waited. Even when the ability to dethrone Saul fell right into David's lap, he refused. David waited, and in this waiting not only was his character developed, but his influence as well. The people in the cave that day saw a man fully trusting in the Lord and not himself, and they knew they could follow a king like that anywhere.

I am aware that in many cases, you, the reader, have seen these things to be true in your own life. You've learned the issue of patience through experience, leadership books, and leadership conferences. Yet how are you instilling these truths in your emerging young leaders? Are you simply frustrated with their impatience? Have you given up? Or are you seeking to lovingly grow your young leaders in the wonders of patience? This is a tricky issue to try to grow in the hearts and lives of young leaders because of their eagerness to move. Much of what I've said in previous chapters may be hard to reconcile with this issue of patience because I'm challenging leaders to give more voice, more dreams, and more influence earlier than they may have received. In my experience, those "giving over" areas enforce and help further patience. The young leaders around us still have to earn trust and prove they are worth following. This takes time and patience.

When the young leaders share with you, their leader, their frustration at the slow acceptance or desire to move from those they lead in their departments or ministries, you can teach them about patience and help equip them to live into patience. Leaders can discuss with their younger leaders how lovingly waiting and not pushing too hard too fast will gain them clout with people. It will allow others (when ready) to develop such trust in them, the young leader, that they will be more apt to move when the correct time rolls around. This is why it is so important that you allow the young leaders to develop trust with those in the organization. Once leaders unleash those in the emerging generations in the fullness of their calling, the young leaders will have learned this lesson early. If the young leaders are to be unleashed in a stronger capacity, your church or organization will have already done the legwork of proving their leadership.

I have earned trust and authority in my current church because leadership has given me a platform with our people and has allowed me to prove my worth. I've been there nine years. It has taken time for me to gain this authority and trust, but I now know I have it in spades with the people of our church. This couldn't have been possible without my leadership's willingness to walk me through these ideas of patience and giving over of influence. Those ingredients have helped me become a better leader in our church, one who is trusted and respected.

If leaders are to unleash the young leaders in their midst in the future, we must equip them with influence *now*. The cost to us as leaders is that in the process, we may sacrifice some of our own influence. This is where the rubber meets the road. Is their future leadership worth diminishing some of our leadership influence today? In my experience, most leaders will say no to that question, and that is a sad reality of leadership. This creates a dangerous atmosphere for future leaders to step into. Without being properly equipped, most young leaders will flounder. Most likely the young leaders, like you and older leaders alike, will land on their feet, but why not set them up for quick success, so they can take the church or organization to heights you couldn't or wouldn't? When we get to part 3 on releasing, we will talk about what the full cost of giving influence will be for you, the older leader. We can't simply equip them in it. We have to give them some of ours. Consider this a pep and prep talk for that section. James Allen said it right: "There is no progress without sacrifice."[49] When we leave our places of leadership, whether by death or by resignation, what legacy do we desire to leave? *As leaders, our greatest legacy is in the success or failure of the future leaders we develop.*

Influence is something earned, something worth waiting for and working for. Will we be leaders who help encourage this in our emerging leaders or not? The choice is up to us. Let me leave this issue of developing influence with two final thoughts: celebrate their wins and encourage them in their losses.

Celebrate the Wins of Your Young Leaders

In the third year of Aletheia (the college church I am leading), I was blessed to baptize five young adults. That was an incredible year of students coming to Christ and recognizing their need to follow Jesus into the waters of baptism. When I reported this news to our home church, the celebration was incredible. The leadership was so excited about this that they asked our media team to make a video celebrating what God was doing at Aletheia and on the University of Pittsburgh's campus. The media team and I went right to work developing the video for the home church to see, so they could hear the great news of new believers and declarations of faith through baptism. Each of the five services at Allegheny Center Alliance Church erupted with applause after the clip was shown. Celebration for the win of the gospel and the work my team and I were doing was an incredible boost. This public display of celebration also allowed our church to see that God was using our efforts at Pitt and that God was using me to be a part of it. That public celebration brought a lot of influence my way. Celebrating the wins of our younger leaders is important to developing influence within any church or organization. A great leader named Nehemiah would agree.

> When it was time for the dedication of Jerusalem's wall, they sought out the Levites in all the places where they lived in order to bring them to

Jerusalem to celebrate the dedication with joy, with thanks and singing, and with cymbals, harps, and lyres. (Nehemiah 12:27)

Leaders should always take time to celebrate when things go right for their young leaders. There must be a celebration when they come to the completion of a project and see what the Lord has done. It's really inspiring to see the excitement that Nehemiah and the people had when the wall was successfully rebuilt. Not only was the wall built, but God also changed the hearts of the people through the building of the wall. That more than anything was worth celebrating. I have experienced in the church a lack of celebration for what God does. Too often we chalk it up as normative and ignore the wins that God sends our way or the way of our young leaders. I think this is wrong, and I enjoy seeing the confirmation of that stance here in the Book of Nehemiah. I believe that we as leaders need to be more positive and find wins (not making them up, mind you, but real live wins) when and where we can and then celebrate them. When leaders start celebrating what God is doing and has done, the people and our young leaders will be spurred on and reignited. When celebration happens under our leadership, our young leaders will remember the God task they are on while following the leader.

I often say to my leadership team that I am excited during our church services because I desire to spur our people on through my excitement: if I'm excited, they'll be excited. But on the other hand, if I'm not excited, they won't be either. Celebrating wins helps leaders to be excited. In turn, their flame of excitement will ignite others around them, and the work of God can advance all the more. When we can celebrate the wins of our young leaders *in front of the people we lead,* both sets of people will be encouraged, and we will begin the deeper process of equipping in influence.

Here is a list of the five ways to celebrate the wins of younger leaders.

1. Have the main leader publicly recognize the win of a younger leader.
2. Celebrate by throwing a dinner or coffee party in the person's honor.
3. Have the main leaders share how grateful they are for the young leader and describe the win in a newsletter or company-wide email.
4. Give opportunity for others in the organization during a meeting (or something similar) to share with the young leader how excited they are for the win.
5. Give public awards to your monthly high-achievers.

Encourage Them in Their Defeats

The idea of encouragement during and after a defeat is pretty straightforward, but that doesn't mean it is often employed. Character is developed through losses, as we've previously discussed, but encouragement in the midst of that loss helps the young leader gain more confidence and influence. When this type of encouragement is present, young leaders won't feel as if they are a failure or that they have failed their leader. Leaders need to pinpoint the faults, but also encourage the young leaders when they have a loss or a failure. This will help spur the young leaders in our midst to continue on and not fall into the trap of self-doubt. Once we equip our young leaders in influence, we can then help equip them in vision. After all, a leader can't cast vision and direction without influence.

Here is a list of the five ways to encourage younger leaders in their defeats:

1. Listen to their frustrations with the defeat and give them space to discuss aloud why they feel it occurred. (Don't try to fix.)
2. Ensure you as their leader help younger leaders to recognize *they* are not failures.
3. Don't let younger leaders quit. In a public forum, share your confidence in them and their leadership.
4. Seek to find a task that you are sure they can greatly succeed in and give it to them.
5. Continue to highlight their strengths and praise them whenever you can.

CHAPTER 7

DEVELOPING VISION

Great Leaders . . . are both highly visionary and highly practical. Their vision enables them to see beyond the immediate.
—John Maxwell[50]

The leader must also live the vision. The leader's effective modeling of the vision makes the picture come alive!
—John Maxwell[51]

When there's no vision, the people get out of control, but whoever obeys instruction is happy. (Proverbs 29:18)

In my first pastorate, I remember a moment when I first walked into my new office. I sat down in my office chair and began thinking, *I have arrived. My hard work in college has paid off. I am now a pastor.* As I sat there thinking those thoughts, a bigger, more looming thought came to mind: *What is my vision for this ministry?* Right away my next thought was, *How and where do I begin?* When those thoughts came, I grabbed my journal and simply wrote, "I need your help, Lord. I have no idea what I'm doing." Although I had learned how to develop a mission and vision statement during my college years, I still had a hard time. The vision statement I developed in college was a generality. Now I had to develop a specific vision for a specific ministry. I was stumped and would spend much of that first year stumbling around with the vision and mission of my new ministry. As I talk with younger leaders who have just stepped into ministry, they, too, experience the same type of difficulty as it pertains to vision.

Vision is much like a compass on a trip. It helps determine and maintain the direction of a course. Anything that would seek to take the trip off course is subject to the vision. A detour to the east will hinder a course due north. The pilot, following the compass, has an easier time of determining whether a direction will help or hinder the trip. Vision is the same. Everything is subject to the vision. It becomes easier for a leader to determine what will hinder or help the direction of the organization based on the vision. *A solid vision gives laser focus, but a weak vision is open to interpretation.* Visions that are open for interpretation are a leader's worst nightmare because everything can contend for time or course direction.

If there is no vision, people will go off and do their own thing, and churches and organizations will flounder. There must be a unifying vision or there will be no movement. The apostle John in the Book of Revelation shares with the church in Ephesus how they were doing so many things well, but they had lost the focus and vision of their first love. This loss of vision caused them to flounder and become ineffective. In Revelation 2:2-5, John urged them to get back to the vision. As well-trained, longtime leaders, you know these truths to be true, not only from a book-knowledge perspective, but also from a very real, experience-driven perspective. As a leader, you've probably experienced several people trying to develop their own vision to help determine the course of your church or organization. You may have inherited a bad vision that continued to get derailed because of its weak nature. As a leader, you know a good vision can be an anchor, so when detractors among your people try to steer the ship off course, you, the leader, can point back to the vision and ask, "Does this direction fit our current vision?" When a vision is strong, that question can be answered with effectiveness. People will be forced to easily recognize if their course correction is in line with the vision or not. If such a vision does not exist, the person will easily be able to persuade others that it does, in fact, fit the overall vision. In order to help young leaders develop a vision, we must ensure they know the imperative nature of a powerful vision.

When it comes to vision, not many young leaders think of vision as a powerful tool in a leader's toolbox. Many times, vision is a "what can be" type of statement, and so it ends up seeming to be simply wishful thinking when many young emerging leaders attempt to develop a vision. Said another way, when young leaders seek to develop a vision, it is too focused on the future and has little focus on the present. This wishful-thinking approach then frustrates many older leaders (maybe even yourself) because it seems easily foiled or lacks practical and tangible steps to be employed right away. A future-only vision also appears to have no real anchor to hold it down. Many times, a younger leader's futuristic vision may be very ambitious and quite possibly out of reach. Often this leads to older leaders looking at the younger leader's vision and saying, "You have no idea how much work that will take. Who's going to do that, you?" However frustrating this may be, there is a gem in this for young emerging leaders—they dream big and have a pretty accurate view of what can be. They may not seem to yet have the ability to pull it off, and the vision may seem a bit open-ended, but if a leader looks at a vision from a future-impacting perspective, they may find out it is something that *could* be . . . and maybe even something that *should* be.

Scott Chrostek, a fellow author in this series with Burlap and Abingdon Press, says this: "The members of the emerging generations that I have encountered have been equipped to see things others cannot. They have a way of grasping the big picture when others are unable. The problem is that they do not know how to effectively make change. This doesn't make them entitled or opinionated, it makes them human."[52]

This statement hits the nail on the head and is important for leaders today to grasp. The implication of this truth is that we as leaders who are on the quest to unleash the emerging generation of leaders must seek to help them develop their vision. We need to help them capture the importance of a *personal* vision as well as a *corporate* vision. They may be able to see the things that can or should be, but we can help emerging leaders develop a vision that not only envisions the future but also anticipates the present. Good visions are forward thinking, with present action steps.

I mentioned that as leaders, we are called to help them develop personal and corporate visions because many a leader fails without a vision for themselves. Who are they called to be? What is their vision for their life and their future? Too much focus goes into the vision of the church or corporation and not the leaders themselves. Many young leaders, without this anchor of a personal vision, may end up taking on jobs they are not meant for. The young leader may end up trying to do too much and be diminished in the process. When a leader is alive, so is the church or organization that person is leading. Without a personal vision, young leaders will have no anchoring point to help them say no to certain things or yes to others. Then, once they have grappled with and developed a personal vision, they can jump into developing a church, ministry, or corporate vision. When those two visions are aligned, it is a powerful sight to see. If leaders feel drained one hundred percent of the time from the vision they helped develop, they will eventually feel stuck and bitter. Yet when the vision of the church or organization they lead excites them because it resonates with them and their personal vision, that will be a powerful leader.

Many young leaders have a wanderlust mentality. We see this through the statistics, where we notice that millennial men and women do not stay long at one job or even live in one place too long. There is a sense of mystery and a rejection of the longevity of their forebears. When asked about this rejection of longevity, many of the young adults I work with state they do not want to live out their lives hating a job that they went into because of the money or convenience, as previous generations did. *Millennials do not reject longevity. They reject prolonged languishing in jobs they detest.*[53] Those in the emerging generations do not want to end up as they saw their parents or grandparents—tired and beat up from a job they hated or doing a job they felt drained by.

The idea of personal vision may have been needed with the previous generations as well. Maybe they could've chosen careers that gave life rather than stole life. Millennials know they desire careers and roles that give life instead of taking it, and they search for it through "job shopping." However, I firmly believe that if we can have these talented, young, lively leaders put together a personal vision plan, they will see more easily what they were built to do. I hope I've established this enough in the earlier part of the book: young leaders who know a leader knows them and has their best in mind will *want* that leader to help develop their personal visions. Scott Chrostek echoes this as well when he states, "The emerging generations need the influence and mentorship of the generations that have gone before . . . the emerging generations covet these types of relationships."[54]

Personal Vision

A personal vision statement puts one's personal calling in a succinct sentence. I discussed the need for leaders to help emerging leaders lean into their calling in the previous chapter, so there is no need to rehash that, but it helps to have the knowledge before a leader can help a person in the emerging generation develop a personal vision. So, here I will build upon the calling portion and translate it into a vision statement. As a Christian leader, I fully believe that our true calling can only be discerned through prayer and revelation from the Holy Spirit. As leaders of young leaders, we must seek to help them discern their calling and thus their vision. We may be the only older person in their lives to walk them through this. Again, within the beauty of taking time to first know them, we can more easily discern who they are, what they were made to do, and what their possible calling may be. Those in the emerging generations will also be more open to listening to our advice because of the time we've taken to know them.

The important place to begin is by discussing what vision is. Leaders should begin by sharing their own vision for their lives, as well as how God helped them develop the vision for the church or organization they lead. In these descriptions, it is imperative that leaders teach them the value and heavy weight a vision plays in the life of a person as well as the organization. The leader should then ask, *"Do you have a personal vision for your life?"*—again coming to the wonderful power of questions. You will find that many times those in the emerging generations will not have even thought about a personal vision for their lives.

When I asked my group of Monday-night guys the question of personal vision, they were momentarily stunned because it wasn't a question they had ever thought about. We had discussed calling and what they had felt their calling in life was, but to narrow it down to a statement seemed daunting. One of the guys asked me, "Why is this important?" That question gave me an opportunity to help frame the importance of a personal vision. Personal visions, just like corporate ones, not only help us say yes to that which we need to say yes to in life, but it also helps us determine what we are to say no to. This can be relationships, jobs, practices, habits, addictions . . . you name it. The vision statement of our lives can test all. I let my group of young men know up-front that the personal vision for their lives may vary slightly from season to season in their lives, but generally, it is a constant compass pointing the way for the course of their lives and their ability to live into their calling.

When I shared this, they were eager to know my vision statement, so they could better understand how to frame their own personal vision statements. I jokingly told them I didn't offer it first because I didn't want them to copy my vision. I then shared my personal vision: "I desire to be a husband, father, and pastor who seeks to know God, to be known by God, and who makes God known." I shared with these guys that I put the word *husband* first because I desire to love my wife second only to God. I will say no to things that would overexert me and hinder my marriage. I shared with these young men that I put *father* next because my kids are third on the list of importance, and if what I am saying yes or no to will hinder my ability to be a good father, I will not do it. Finally, *ministry* is listed because it is a part of who I am and my calling, but it is fourth on the list. Then I took time to share with these men why I listed the three aspects of *know, be known,* and *make known.* In all three of my roles, I desire to consistently do and balance these three aspects. If my doing exceeds my knowing, being known, or making God known, I must cut back. If a ministry position arises that I feel called to, I need to check and see if it will allow me to do the three things I am desiring to do with my life. If it doesn't, I shouldn't take that position.

Vision is the lens all leaders should use to determine what they are doing, how they are doing it, and many times when they do it. If what we as leaders are doing does not align with our vision, it should no longer be done. The personal vision then is a blueprint of what leaders are to be doing with their lives. If things are not being done that need to be done, based on the leader's personal vision, the leader needs to adjust. If there are things that are not as important to fulfilling the vision, the leader needs to adjust.

The idea of a personal vision is vital to emerging leaders because it will help them develop a grid to determine which jobs they take and which ones they don't. A personal vision will help those in the emerging generation live into longevity, rather than seeking new thing after new thing. A personal vision will help anchor emerging leaders and give them the ability to have long-term results in the jobs/ministries they seek to lead. A personal vision will also save us as leaders a lot of time, so we are not training the young leaders we lead in something they will eventually walk away from due to a lack of self-knowledge. This takes us back to part 1 of this book, because while we are knowing them and they are knowing us, they will discover new self-revelations that will help you and them work to develop calling and vision. I must again reiterate the importance of *not moving in assumptions; you will find with many in the emerging generations that our assumptions are almost always going to be wrong, if we haven't taken the time to truly know them.*

Corporate Vision

Just as in developing a personal vision, developing a corporate vision requires knowledge. In order to effectively develop a corporate vision that will enliven the people we lead rather than deaden them, we must know them and the organization well. If we come in and ignorantly demand a vision that doesn't fit the organization or the people of the organization, we will be in trouble. If we feel a sense of calling to take the organization or church in a new direction, we must first gain influential capital as well as teach and lead our people to a new season with a new vision. This can't be done too rapidly, or quite frankly, too slowly. This is where it is most vital we develop vision in our young leaders. Our stories of failure in this area are key as well. Sharing failures humanizes us, but it also tells a more compelling lesson.

In my one-on-ones with my lead pastor (as I mentioned before), I ask about his failures as well as triumphs. I have found for myself that I learn more from his stories of failure than his triumphs. I know the same is true in the young leaders I mentor and make disciples of. This also reiterates that failure is more than OK—it is necessary for ongoing growth and development.

When it comes to vision, we must seek to instill patience in our young leaders and allow them to get to know those whom they are seeking to direct with a vision for a ministry, church, or organization. *Premature vision can be as detrimental as a wrong vision.*

Young leaders will amaze you with their ability to capture the heart of a church or organization quickly, but they will still need help putting a practical vision together. This means we have to leave room for them to vision cast aloud with us, so we can assist in honing the vision they see as a possibility. We can't simply teach them about vision; we need to let them cast vision. This, more than anything, will help us develop them in vision. It will help us to see what they see and will give us insight on where they need help developing vision.

This begins within their perspective areas of leadership. Let them develop a vision. Ask them questions about their area of leadership, about the people they lead, and the potential strengths and weaknesses of their area. Discuss their personal vision to see how it aligns with their current area of leadership. Once they give you the vision, help them see potential pitfalls with the vision and explain how that vision may or may not be received.

Once you are satisfied that they have come up with a significant, succinct, and strong vision, let them run with it in their area of leadership. Unleash them along with their vision. Give them authority to lead from this vision. If people under their leadership have issues, help handle the objections. After all, you were an integral part of the visioning process. This unleashing of authority will encourage young leaders, who will own the vision in a way that they wouldn't if it weren't their vision. I firmly believe that all young leaders need to be released to do this within their perspective areas of leadership. This will give them an edge when they are fully unleashed to lead on their own, with their own authority, because they will have experienced the whole process from concept to execution.

I would encourage you not to stop there, however. Just as I stated the importance of letting emerging leaders dream, we must let them cast vision—not just for their own areas of leadership, but also for the whole organization as well. Seek their advice and opinions on the vision for your church or organization. See what they are seeing, which you may not be seeing. This falls in line with being teachable. I cannot emphasize this enough throughout the book—when we give younger leaders a voice into the organization as a whole, they will feel valued. Young emerging leaders who feel valued will be all in. When a young leader is all in, we as older leaders receive the benefits of their energy and passion. It's true what they say about us older leaders. We tend to be less energetic, less passionate, and more cynical than we used to be. Unleashing the young emerging leaders in our midst to cast vision will enliven our vision and reignite a passion we may have allowed to dwindle. Again, I think we can turn to the great leader Nehemiah for a powerful example of vision casting.

Leaders Cast Vision (Nehemiah 2:17)

"So I said to them, 'You see the trouble that we're in: Jerusalem is in ruins, and its gates are destroyed by fire! Come, let's rebuild the wall of Jerusalem so that we won't continue to be in disgrace!'" (Nehemiah 2:17)

Nehemiah took the time to assess the situation, he took the time to care about his people, and he *took the time to pray to ask God what must be done.* Finally, he is ready to cast the vision to the people and get them on board with the mission. His steps were deliberate and wise. He didn't rush into telling them what must be done and how he, Nehemiah, was going to do it. He took the time to patiently seek the Lord and to patiently see what ought to be done and think through how best to get it done. He cast vision, but not prematurely, and in a way that rallied the people around the vision.

Wilkes says, "Leadership begins when a God-revealed mission captures a person."[55] I believe that the God-revealed mission captured Nehemiah and he was ready to start working on the rebuilding of the wall. Once captured by the vision, he could perfectly articulate that vision to the people and speak of it in such a way that people could see the end result. It's as Wilkes said of Jesus: "Jesus articulated his mission in order to define what he was as Messiah. Where and how he led flowed from a clear sense of why he had come in the first place . . . he led with a vision of what things would look like when he completed that mission."[56]

I briefly discussed my belief that a vision is most powerful when discerned through prayer and the Spirit. As a believer and a pastor, I can't develop a vision without the help of the Holy Spirit. If I do, it will be subject to the attacks of the enemy and will not be the stout, resolute vision it must be, especially a vision for a ministry, church, or Christian organization. Jesus *must* be the center and must be the anchor. It can be easy to become "corporate Christians," where our meetings, agendas, and visions are done more with a business mind-set than a dependent-upon-the-Spirit mind-set. Staff meetings become about the agenda, with little to no prayer. We lead with less and less power and authority when we neglect to leave room for the Spirit to move, breathe, and for God to have God's way. Nehemiah was a leader who prayed and spent time seeking the heart of God. Even if the vision God gives seems to be unattainable or will surely be a tough road to get others on board with, it is a vision that must be followed. I desired to end with this in mind because we generally remember the last things we read more so than the first things we read (unless they supremely resonate with us, that is).

Leading with dependence on the Holy Spirit displays a powerful lesson to our emerging leaders—leadership is not about us, especially leadership within a ministry setting. Too often, when we neglect the Spirit, we end up making monuments to our leadership and ourselves. We may even have our organization be driven by our personality. This will end up hindering the emerging generation instead of helping. If God is the one in charge, casting vision, and if we are allowing the leaders in our midst to have a voice, cast vision, share dreams, and lead well, we release our grip on our own importance. However, before we can teach or help develop someone in a certain area, we must first be living it ourselves.

So, as we end this chapter, let me ask you a few questions:

Are you giving room for your emerging leaders to think of vision?

Are you helping them hone their visions?

Are you allowing them to show you things you may not see?

Are you giving them the tools to cast the vision?

Finally, are you leading through dependence on the Holy Spirit to cast your vision? When I ask this question of myself, I look through a grid of three ways I think of to assist in leading through dependence on the Holy Spirit.

Grid of Three Ways to Lead Through Dependence

1. **Prayer**—Spending time in prayer and seeking the Lord for vision not only postures us to hear better from God, but also displays our admittance that we need God's voice to develop vision.

2. **Discernment**—Spending time in prayer will give us opportunity to discern the will of the Lord as it pertains to personal and corporate vision. It is incumbent on the leaders then to test what they hear through the lens of discernment. This can be done by testing against Scripture as well as seeking input from discerning people in the life of the leader.

3. **Obedience**—Once the leaders hear from the Lord, they must then obey and follow through.

Your answers to the above questions should've exposed you to where you are with dependence. God has placed us in roles of leadership over our emerging leaders for a reason. The reason is to know, equip, and release them for leadership. We cannot do that effectively without the leading of the Holy Spirit or without giving them opportunities to develop and then cast vision. Let's move into one last "technical" development—developing communication—so that we can train them to best release the vision they are developing with the help of the Spirit and ourselves.

CHAPTER 8

DEVELOPING COMMUNICATION

One of the most powerful agents of change in reaching people is our words.
—Steve Saccone[57]

Communication in today's world is light-years different from the world of yesterday. Today, communication is not just in the form of public speaking or written form, as in a book; communication is found in several different mediums. Social media, for example, has changed the game on how to not only communicate and keep in touch, but also on how to disseminate information. We are living in a society that is saturated in media, information, and communication. Maybe as you were looking ahead to this chapter, you were realizing your own need to learn how to best communicate in such a society. Whether you were or weren't hoping to glean that from this chapter, the very real truth is this: we need to effectively communicate if we are to lead, and our emerging leaders also need to communicate with efficiency and effectiveness if they are to succeed. With all these new mediums of communication, we must find a way to have a voice and lead others well by good, strong communication.

How can we develop communication in our emerging leaders to the degree that those who follow them understand what's being said and then can translate that into action? As I sit to write this chapter, that is the very question I plan to answer. In order to answer that question well, we have to look at specific mediums of communication and how to effectively communicate for each medium; although the principles may be similar, the method, approach, and thought that go into the communication will be different. Here are the microcosmic mediums we will look at: Digital Communication, Personal Communication, and Communication in Meetings.

Digital Communication

This one area of communication will either be the breakthrough or breakdown for our young leaders as they communicate with their generation and the generations behind them. The current digitization of communication has increased information, consumption, and even the stupidity of how people give and receive communication. Much of the communication that currently happens on the differing social media platforms is either toxic or vague. This creates space for horrendous debates and misconstrued intentions. This type of dialogue, rather than fostering relationship, mutual learning, and communal understanding, ends up far too often making relationships split due to differing views or wounded pride based on toxic debate. Many older generation leaders simply choose not to engage on these platforms—and I think that is to their detriment. Not only are they not helping make these social media platforms healthier, but they also are unable to mentor their younger leaders on how to best approach this form of communication.

In my own personal experience, I have posted things that infuriated people, caused people to rejoice with my ability to articulate well a social issue, and everything in between. Through each of these exchanges, I've learned many things about what to do and what not to do in digital communication as it pertains to social media platforms. Many times those seeking to grow me have rebuked me, and I was able to see the rebuke actually had merit. The first thing we must instill in our young leaders is this: *Pray before you post.*

Much of the stupidity that goes on in the social media world is due to quick reactions and thoughtless verbal vomit. Many of the issues that arise due to such careless posting could be avoided with a simple deep breath and a prayer for wisdom on what to say (if anything). When employing this myself, I have found I end up not posting what I originally desired to post, if I post anything at all. *Reactionary communication never ends well.* We must be people who seek to respond with grace and truth, always ensuring the relationship is more important than our opinions. When we invite God into the process of our communication, things turn out better. This is a hard lesson for younger emerging leaders. They've grown up with this type of technology. They are digital natives, and this flow of opinionated communication is what most of them have been developing. As the older leaders, we must seek to share with them the importance of relationships over opinions, as well as the lesson on prayer before posting.

The next thing we must instill in our young emerging leaders when it comes to social media digital communication is the importance of *knowing whom you represent*. This was the hardest lesson for me personally to capture. I felt entitled to post whatever I desired to post because it was my personal blog, my personal Facebook page, or my personal Twitter. However, the majority of people who follow me on these social media outlets know where I work and what I do. As a pastor, I do not have the luxury of simply representing myself. I represent the church in many ways as well. I will be honest: I hated this reality and in my individuality still dislike the concept. However, whether I like it or not, it is true. Young leaders, especially those who lead within the church, must come to grips with this fact. It is interesting to me how hypocritical I and many other people my age are about this issue. When our current president uses Twitter (as he is known to do) and makes outrageous statements, we immediately state something along the lines of this: "You represent America. That does not represent my values or American values." Yet we don't want to own the responsibility of our own actions on social media being representative of the churches or companies we represent.

As we continue down the road of developing communication in the digital realm, we must also instill in our young leaders the importance of *choosing the right hills*. When it comes to opinions or topics to bring forth for discussion or heated argument, the options are endless. Too often, the social issues that tend to rapidly come up in our nation these days are the main themes of social media posting. Everyone has an opinion, and many times, people purposefully bait others to get reactionary responses. Helping our young leaders discern which hills are vital to fight on and which ones are just plain useless is key to digital communication. Prayer will definitely help in this discernment process, but so will discussing church or organizational values that are important, so when they represent the church, they can do it with those values in mind. This will help our young leaders to know better which issues the church or organization would tackle and then go all in (with truth, grace, and love) to those discussions. It's as I said: these online conversations are going to be of great importance to our future leaders. The media platform may shift from Facebook, Twitter, Snapchat, Instagram, or whatever, to the next thing down the line, but there will always be a next thing. Having our young emerging leaders learn these lessons now will help them tremendously when they are fully unleashed into the leadership role they are ultimately called to.

Finally, we cannot ignore the digital communication done through text-messaging. Texting is one of the main forms/modes of communication among the millennial and Z generations. Phone calls and emails are no longer the first (sometimes not even the second or third) line of communication. Many of my college students only use email to connect with bosses or professors. They have all sorts of different methods for some sort of text-messaging they primarily use. There is the typical text-messaging, but there is also Facebook messaging, GroupMe, and several others; Snapchat is also a form of text-messaging (just with pictures). The danger in communicating serious issues via text is the issue of being misunderstood. The temptation is to text about serious or complicated issues because that is the main mode of communication for our young leaders. Yet we must train them to understand that this will not be the best way to communicate, articulate, or work through larger issues. I have seen many relationships suffer due to these miscommunications that occur over text-messaging. If I'm honest, I've failed to realize the pitfalls of texting about serious issues.

Training our young leaders on this can be as simple as how we respond when they text us about a complex issue. In that moment, we should say, "Call me, so we can work this out outside of texts" or "Let's discuss this tomorrow in person." The temptation for us will be to address it then in the text-message, but we should not give into this temptation. Once we've suggested that new time of face-to-face or over-the-phone communication, we can encourage them to do the same with those they are leading. When they come to us with frustration over being misunderstood, seek to see if this happened due to digital communication rather than face-to-face or over the phone. Many times in my experience, the misunderstanding or miscommunication will have happened via digital communication rather than the other two ways of communication, and we can leverage those times as a teachable moment.

With digital communication, the same rules apply as with social media—pray before you post, know who you represent, and choose the right hills. Once a text is sent, it has the capability of being there, on the other person's phone, indefinitely. That person can keep going back to it and stewing on it because it is in written form. Praying before we text and choosing the right hills will go a long way toward establishing healthy, stronger communication.

Personal Communication

A key to helping young emerging leaders better communicate on a personal level is to challenge them to listen more than they speak. I confess I am also speaking to myself when I write this advice. As a younger, more energetic person, I tend to speak twice as much as I listen. This tendency has gotten me in more trouble than I could even remember. With my wife, my friends, my coworkers, my bosses, and those following me, I have seen this time and time again negatively affect my ability to not only communicate but also to lead effectively. Communication is not just speaking. It is listening, soaking in what the other person is saying, and then digesting it. If our goal in leadership is to be the loudest, most important, and/or only voice heard, we are in for a rough road. In that, I am speaking to the choir, to you, an older leader. These are lessons I am sure you've already learned. Yet we must seek to imprint this truth in our younger leaders.

Maybe give them a monthly challenge of a day of silence, when they are forced to cease talking for one day a month, so they can practice the art of listening. Then debrief the experience with them. I think they will find it both rough and rewarding. However, I think you can ingrain this truth into the emerging generation of leaders in a loving, convicting way. Again, because I personally struggle with this (just ask my wife), I see the utter importance of helping our younger leaders wrestle with it as soon as possible. Good leaders listen. Personally, I've learned to utilize five ways to employ better listening:

1. Listen to hear, not to respond.
2. Put my cell phone away and do not look at it during my conversation.
3. Repeat back to the speaker what was said to ensure I heard properly.
4. Maintain eye contact and do not become easily distracted.
5. Speak half as much as I listen.

The reason this can be so difficult goes back to the issue of entitlement for many in the upcoming generations. Entitlement says my voice is the most important. That sense of entitlement can be detrimental to personal communication with others. Here again, we can use the power of good questions to help our young leaders recognize why they talk more than they listen (if, in fact, they do).

Lastly, in line with listening in personal communication, training our younger leaders to listen to learn is vitally important. Many times, those in the millennial and Z generations tend to want to only share their opinions. They go into a conversation with what they want to say and ignore what the other person is saying. There is also the tendency to listen just to say they listened, but not to seek to learn. When we can listen with a heart of humility, rather than arrogance, the people we are communicating with will have an easier time listening to us. If we ignore them and communicate with them just so they can hear what we have to say, we fail to properly communicate. Impress on your young leaders that communication is a two-way street.

Communication in Meetings

Meetings can be exciting or boring. Sadly, most are boring, but they don't have to be. Most of the boredom occurs due to poorly executed agendas or drab communication of the items on the agenda. As a younger leader and as one who leads younger leaders, I know that meetings are not generally looked upon favorably, but they are great opportunities to allow the younger leader's voice to be heard by the people present. Whether it is a staff meeting, donor meeting, congressional meeting, or board meeting, it can be a great opening for a young leader to be heard.

In order to help our young leaders to be heard, however, we must give them tools to effectively communicate to those listening. One of the key issues we must train them in is *knowing the audience*. As you are aware, our knowledge of the audience we are seeking to lead is vital to getting our points across. If we can't translate the necessary actions or areas of learning to those we are leading, it generally is because we failed to know how our audience would receive the information we were giving. Young leaders may or may not get the importance of this. I know many young leaders who were frustrated because they were not heard or understood. They were unaware of how to say what needed to be said for their audience to hear it. Audiences change, and so the way we communicate will vary from group to group.

I saw this happen early on in my ministry. I was the associate/youth pastor at my first church, but my main task was the youth ministry. I loved being a youth pastor and knew my middle school and high school audience well. However, I had *no clue* how to talk to parents, especially how to talk to parents about their children. In my youthful arrogance, as a twenty-one-year-old, I attempted to teach parents of teenagers how to raise their kids. I remember one parent meeting, when I got into an argument with the parent of a middle school student about his readiness to go on a missions trip to Africa. I was ill-prepared to speak to this audience, and it was painfully obvious that I needed to quickly understand how to speak to them well. Thankfully, the ministry college I graduated from was in the same town, and one of my youth ministry professors was also a youth leader. I quickly begged him to give me insight on communicating well with parents.

Since we want to set these young leaders up well for successful leadership presently and in the future, we must take time to explain our audience. We must also give them the tools of organization and authority. A meeting can be derailed by a loosey-goosey agenda, so developing an organized, specific agenda is key to communicating well. Otherwise, it can get bogged down or derailed, and the information that was supposed to be communicated will be lost. Sadly, even with a strong agenda, things can get off course, and that is why I also mentioned authority. An authoritative leader can effectively bring the discussion back on course. That person can lovingly draw the meeting back to the main points, and people will go there with that leader because of the authority wielded. This authority, however, is developed and earned.

As leaders seeking to unleash these young emerging leaders, we must give them authority and train them how best to use it. We must purposefully set aside time in meetings to give them voice and to give them the opportunity to earn the authority so needed in leadership. This trains them to gain authority within the group they are leading, so when they go out of our church or organization, they are equipped with the skills to quickly gain the authority needed in order to be an effective leader. Much of these tools can be used for platform communication as well.

Part 3
Releasing

CHAPTER 9

THE CALL TO FLOURISHING

When leaders seek to see younger leaders flourish, they are also seeking the success of the future of their organization. The younger leaders' success will be a picture of our ability to help them flourish. Their failure will be a reflection of our inability to help them flourish. Their flourishing should be a top priority in our sending them out into their own roles or even as we apprentice them to take ours. We can leave a legacy through our young leaders or we can leave a stalled movement. I believe every one of you reading this book would choose to leave behind a legacy rather than a stalled movement.

Leaving a legacy means that the leaders who follow us continue on the work we've done and improve upon it. Legacy in the long view of things is not about us at all. Legacy is about leaving behind something that remains in motion, and this is through the future leaders. This view of flourishing and legacy was something King Saul missed in his leadership.

Saul loved the spotlight. He loved the accolades that were poured onto him as king. Saul loved power, prestige, and suck-ups. Anything or anyone that made him inferior was something to be pounced on like a lion. He didn't want to be outshone, nor did he desire to share the glory with any man . . . or even with God. He took credit, owned the glory for himself, and tried to kill those who attempted to interfere with his glory. This was the case with David. Saul at first was relieved when David showed up on the scene. David killed Goliath, but when David started gaining more fans, Saul got could not contain the real, selfish king he truly was.

And the women sang to one another as they celebrated,

"Saul has struck down his thousands,
    and David his ten thousands."

And Saul was very angry, and this saying displeased him. He said, "They have ascribed to David ten thousands, and to me they have ascribed thousands, and what more can he have but the kingdom?" And Saul eyed David from that day on.

And Saul hurled the spear, for he thought, "I will pin David to the wall." But David evaded him twice.

Saul was afraid of David because the LORD was with him but had departed from Saul.

And when Saul saw that he had great success, he stood in fearful awe of him.
(1 Samuel 18:7-9. 11-12, 15, ESV)

Saul had messed up as king, so God had left Saul and stopped giving him favor. Due to Saul's wicked and unrepentant heart, God was forced to choose another king. God chose David and began showering favor upon David. God's Spirit rested upon David. This success infuriated Saul. Instead of celebrating that God was giving Israel a better king, Saul became jealous and sought to end David's life . . . further separating himself from the Lord and the Lord's will.

I will be the first to admit that as a leader, it is sometimes hard to see those under me achieving success. It's hard, not because I'm so great, but because my sinful nature wants to be better than them. We judge ourselves in comparison to others. When we look at our young leaders' status or the accolades being given to them while they are under our leadership, shouldn't we get some credit too? This train of thought begins to take us down a road that desires to choke off their flourishing, rather than seek it out for them.

However, we are jealous of others' success, aren't we? If someone gets promoted over us, we get frustrated, jealous, and bitter sometimes. If someone younger (or less experienced) than us gets more accolades for effort than we do, it makes us freak out because, after all, we've been doing it longer.

Saul sought only his glory, and so he jealously kept all his leadership lessons to himself. There was no attempt to teach a younger guy how to be king. He hated David's success, and the moment it looked like David was more blessed by God and was being prepared to take the throne was the moment Saul literally began to lose his mind. We as leaders need to be seeking how to invest in the future—even if someone eclipses us in the process—especially in the church. It's not about us. It's about God. Saul, as king over Israel, was supposed to be pointing the whole nation to God. Instead, he was trying to point them to himself.

His reign was all about his glory, not God's glory. Saul cared more about his image than he did the image of God. Brothers and sisters, we can't be like Saul. I fail here a ton. I am a people-pleaser, and I want people to like me. I want the glory and the spotlight.

There was a time early in our church plant when I was jealous of my discipleship and worship pastor, Joseph. I knew God had called me to develop him as a preacher/teacher, and so, as I mentioned earlier, I let him know I wanted him to preach one Sunday. I remember him killing it. God used him and his words in a powerful way. Right after he preached, I had one congregant come up to me and say, "He needs to preach more often. Why hasn't he been preaching? I want to hear him more." In my weak, selfish self, I felt hurt by her statement. My ego was so fragile at this time that I thought she was trying to get me to stop preaching altogether. I heard her saying he's better and his voice needs to be heard above yours. She *wasn't* saying that, but I felt as if she were. I had to wrestle with God on this. I had to ask God's Spirit to tame my wild selfishness and allow me to hear what was really being said. I know for a fact if I would've nursed that bitterness, Joseph and I wouldn't be as close as we are now and the enemy would've used that to derail the ministry God has called us to do *together.*

We must die to ourselves and start pointing to God. Our gifts are God's gifts. Our ministry is God's ministry. Our wisdom is God's wisdom. We, my friends, are simply stewards of all God has given us. We don't own anything, not even who we are or our leadership favor. We have no control over who we would be. We simply have a choice to steward that which was given.

Saul failed in developing an apprentice. We should not fail here as well. God has entrusted our leadership roles to us to not only lead now, but also to lead when we're gone. We must look and see: who are the young leaders who have the Lord's anointing on them? How can we pick them out and apprentice them for what God has for them in the future?

True, honest leadership, I'm learning, is leadership that develops others. A strong leader may be effective for thirty or forty years, but a leader who invests in the up-and-comers, celebrates their success, and seeks to make them better . . . that leader is investing in the future and beginning a legacy, rather than keeping the younger leaders in a stalled movement. When we apprentice, our skills and our gifts sometimes get transferred. So even if we die, we are still a part of that younger leader's life. *Our influence goes further than our own life span.* This is amazing to think about. If we seek the flourishing of our younger leaders and we seek to invest in them and give them the best of ourselves, our influence lives beyond ourselves.

This is a concept I must cling to as God uses me to mold and shape young college leaders. My church is predominantly comprised of college students, which means I have approximately two-and-a-half years to develop them before I send them out. I say two-and-a-half years because many first-semester and even second-semester college freshman are not ready to be developed. They are trying to find themselves. So, as they seek to discover who they are, I am a resource, but they are not yet ready to be shaped. By the time they are sophomores, I've found that they are giant sponges. They've figured out the college rhythm and are seeking to be poured into on a higher level. I have the ability then to develop them, train them, challenge them, and watch them grow through their first semester of senior year. I move back into a resource for them because they are seeking to find their place out of college. They begin internships or masters course hunting and purposefully begin to pull away (whether consciously or unconsciously), so when they leave the pain isn't so bad.

Knowing I have these two-and-a-half years of their lives puts me into high gear for development. What needs to be developed in two-and-a-half years? That was my first question as I began this church plant. I found two things that needed to be spoken into them in order for them to flourish: missional flourishing and spiritual flourishing. I believe these two things stretch across all types of churches and Christian organizations.

Missional Flourishing

I hope by now you are seeing how this whole book builds upon itself. We can't call our young leaders to flourish if we don't *know* them, and we can't *release* them unless we *equip* them. All three components—*knowing, equipping,* and *releasing*—flow together and must be built one on top of the other. Releasing the young leaders to flourish is a key component to seeing them unleashed. Part of being a great leader is staying on mission. Many things in life will seek to detract us leaders from the mission, and the enemy of our souls will seek to take us off our God-given mission. As a pastor, much of my missional flourishing, and therefore my understanding of it, stems from church leadership. I think the insights here can be across the board if simply reworded.

With my church, I seek to train the younger generations and then unleash them on mission. Every year-and-a-half, I seek to do a course named after a book titled, *The Tangible Kingdom*. I utilize material from that book as well as another book titled, *Everyday Church,* to impart what I feel is our mission as a church— knowing Christ, being known by Christ, and making God known (yes, this is also my personal vision). *The Tangible Kingdom* course deals primarily with the part of *making God known*. Many times, being on mission needs to be taught, then there needs to be given ample opportunities to live into the mission. Both the teaching and the living into the mission create the optimum space for missional flourishing.

One of the main core themes of living into the mission of our church is living an incarnational life. This simply means we seek to be Christ to our campus. We study the Gospels and see how Christ interacted with the religious people of his day, as well as the outcasts and sinners. Then we seek to be filled with the Holy Spirit, so that we can live as Christ did. I explain that we can do this by purpose-fully placing ourselves among non-Christians so that they can see our lives and then, as 1 Peter 3:15 declares, by asking questions about the hope we have. If we are living an incarnational life, we will be living differently from those around us in our current culture, so they will be compelled to eventually ask us questions about our "different lives."

When we first began this missional flourishing within our church, we started attending a student organization called SLIM (Student Leaders of International Medicine). Their heart aligned with Christ's heart in that they sought to bring medicine to underfunded countries. We could get on board with that mission and live among them as Christ did. Through this one organization, we've seen several students connect with our church and as a result, with Christ. I am still close with one student in particular, who sees me as a second dad. After I mod-eled this, I've seen several of our college (and noncollege) congregants catch this mission and begin to flourish in it themselves. This then set many of the students up for success after the two-and-a-half years they had with me pouring into them. We've seen students head into missions organizations such as Cru (Campus Cru-sade for Christ), as well as Envision (a young adult missions arm of the Christian and Missionary Alliance). We saw the importance of our leaders flourishing in the mission of Christ. We taught them and then unleashed them. In my mind, a mission is not fully understood unless it is lived into. We can help our younger leaders live into the mission by releasing them to do so and giving them opportunities to flourish.

The scary part for us is that they may do so well, we lose our seat of importance. Their flourishing may mean we choose to diminish a little bit, so they can flourish even more. Once we established a presence at SLIM, I bowed out of meetings and allowed some of our other students to lead the way of the mission. This was hard for me, but I know it was necessary for them to flourish. Part of releasing our young leaders is calling them to flourish and then giving them the opportunities to shine. Young leaders can flourish when they see me making the mission more important than myself. Saul couldn't see this, but we must. Leaving a legacy means the emerging generations of leaders catch the mission. If they don't, the mission will be lost in a stagnated movement.

Spiritual Flourishing

I fully believe that the most important area of flourishing for young leaders is their spiritual flourishing. In my opinion, the mission of Christ can't be fully lived out without the empowerment of the Holy Spirit. Some of you reading this may not lead Christian organizations or lead in churches, but I am compelled to discuss the spiritual flourishing of our emerging leaders. I have seen this flourishing in my own life again and again, giving me the wisdom to flourish in other areas of my life, as well as in the lives of my young emerging leaders.

When I was being trained for ministry at my college in Nyack, New York, I learned a lot about ministry, its purposes, and its potential pitfalls. Yet it wasn't until my junior year that I was able to really be ready for the ministry God was calling me to. I arrogantly felt ready before then, but I was wrong. I took a course with my now mentor, Ron Walborn, on building a flourishing spiritual life, and it changed the ball game for me. The course was called Personal Spiritual Formation (PSF). I've mentioned this class in my other books because it has been that influential in my life—I just have to talk about it.

In this class, we saw the importance of becoming emotionally healthy in order to be spiritually healthy. We discussed grieving losses and the importance of honesty, as well as the importance of being known by God. I was able to see the reasons for many of my issues and allow God to do some deep inner healing of my heart and soul. I know for a fact that without the transformational truths I received in this course, I would no longer be in ministry. I would've flunked out and left ministry long ago. It was this spiritual flourishing that has kept me on mission because it taught me the importance of dependence on the Lord and the empowering presence of the Holy Spirit. This is the time in my life I learned the need for surrender. I still struggle with it, obviously, but it was here, as a young emerging leader, that I learned the beginning phases of surrender. All the leadership lessons in the world will not help me without the empowering presence of the Holy Spirit. It is our duty to call our young leaders to flourish spiritually.

Many of my young leaders will be lay leaders in the church, leading and working in several different types of careers, but I still believe they need their spiritual life to flourish. That is why I teach the PSF course to my leaders. I asked Ron for permission to teach his course, and he approved. I've changed some stuff over the years and personalized it, but the core ideas remain the same. I heard the Spirit speak to me early on about the spiritual flourishing of my young (and older) leaders. He said to my heart simply, "Without PSF, your leaders will fail." I was convinced then and even more so now that this is true. I've spent many years walking my leaders through PSF and have seen them flourish in every other area of their lives because they were flourishing in their spiritual lives.

The two main courses I teach over and over again to each round of young leaders are *The Tangible Kingdom* and PSF. I just can't move away from these two courses because I've seen them work and know they will continue to do so. However, as I mentioned in the Missional Flourishing segment, it is not enough to teach PSF; I must give them space to interact with the lessons and put them into practice themselves. I cannot force them. They must want it. The sad thing is this: not every young leader sees the importance of spiritual flourishing, and ignores many of the deep truths spoken about in our PSF course. These leaders learn something new for sure, but it doesn't affect their lives. I watch as they languish under the pressures of life and work that could be a lot lighter if they just surrendered to the King.

The great news is, when my young leaders capture the vision of surrender and put it into practice and begin to apply the truths of Scripture in their spiritual lives, they excel in every other area of life and leadership. It really is an amazing thing to behold. We must call our young leaders to flourish in their walk with Christ. You don't have to teach PSF for this to happen, but find a way to encourage your young leaders to grow in their walks with Christ. Walk alongside them in this. Encourage them, challenge them, and grow with them. If they do not have a flourishing life spiritually, they *will* flounder in the other areas of their lives. Many a young leader has fallen due to a lack of spiritual flourishing. We can be leaders who leave a legacy of healthy leaders in our wake. Churches and organizations will be hungry to grab the leaders we are training because they will see the health and success of the previous leaders we've called to flourish spiritually, and they will desire that type of young leader.

Sadly, I've run into more unhealthy young leaders than healthy ones. In large part, this is due to their lack of spiritual flourishing. These young leaders have never dealt with the issues that plague their core, and so they walk around blind to the land mines that surround them. We, by our lives, must show the importance of spiritual flourishing. We discussed the importance of recognizing our lives are on display, and as Christian leaders, our spiritual health is the most important thing to display to our young emerging leaders, especially those in the church. We can't call our young leaders to spiritual flourishing if we ourselves are not spiritually flourishing. We must grow, so we can help them grow.

The call to flourishing is vital to releasing our young leaders because their flourishing gives us security that when they launch, they will be healthy enough to continue to flourish and to handle the pressures of the role they will be unleashed into. This is the first step to releasing. Once we recognize the flourishing of both the mission and their souls, we can then move into the second step of releasing, and that's the step of giving influence.

CHAPTER 10

GIVING INFLUENCE

When you believe in people, you motivate them and release their potential.
—John Maxwell[58]

YOUNG LEADERS NEED TO FEEL AS IF THEY ARE BELIEVED IN. Much of the child-rearing of the millennial and Z generations had a large component of over-encouragement. There were statements said by family and society such as, "Everyone is a winner. Everyone is special." This caused some in these generations to consistently need affirmation. Some need affirmation so badly that they will shut down if they do not receive it. Those types of leaders, unless they adjust their expectation of both themselves and those they lead, will struggle deeply in leadership or fail altogether. As you know, affirmation is hard to come by in leadership, but it is still important. I begin this chapter with this honest discussion, so you, the reader, don't think I am ignorant of the issues pertaining to millennials and Z generation young leaders as they pertain to affirmation.

When I discuss the idea of giving influence, it can be tempting to see it as another "feeding the beast of affirmation" for these generations. The reality is this: giving influence is needed and should've been provided for you as you moved into leadership. When we discuss giving influence, we must be wary of the generational pitfall that assails many a millennial and Z generation young leader, but not allow that to hinder us from giving influence to young leaders.

One of the best ways to affirm young emerging leaders and the best way to let them know you believe in them is to give them influence. As we discussed in the chapter on "Developing Influence," young leaders need to know how to grow in and utilize their influence. Taking cash out of your leadership influence bank account can help give the young leaders you lead a leg up when it comes to growing in and using their leadership influence. This then sets them up for the best possible release into leadership.

So, if it is so important to give influence to the emerging leaders in our churches or organizations, how do we go about doing this? I know we don't want to lose too much of our personal influence account with our congregation or people in our organizations, so how can we do it well by not losing too much? I will take us through several options to best give influence to the emerging generation of leaders. Know, however, I in no way think this list covers every way possible to give influence to the younger leaders, but I think these ways are good primers for you and your team to develop your own plan on giving influence.

Give Credit

One of the simplest ways to give influence is to give credit where credit is due. I recognize I've mentioned this twice before. I mention it now a third time because it is an area I have seen many older leaders neglect. If you are working closely with a young leader, you give that person an opportunity to share an idea. When you implement the idea, make sure everyone knows whose idea it was. Sometimes we inadvertently take credit, but we must carefully walk through ideas presented and ensure we give the proper person credit. When we share that our young leader had a great idea, we share with the team this person is valuable, and we give them a voice into what we are doing. Also, the fact that you implemented their idea tells the group that your young leader is also worth listening to because that person has great ideas.

The young leader and other young leaders in your church or organization will take note of this and feel heard. This aspect of giving influence doesn't take any cash out of our accounts of influence. It doesn't add cash either. However, it does deposit some fresh cash into the account of the young leader with the great idea.

If for whatever reason you take the credit for the young leader's idea, you lose a lot more than you gain. The young leader will feel betrayed and used. Young leaders will feel somewhat validated in their ability to lend value to the team, but will feel as if their contributions ultimately don't help them or set them up for leadership in the future. Giving credit where it's due makes sense with any person you're working with, but I would say it is even more important for the young leaders you are seeking to develop.

Celebrate Their Wins—Publicly

Young leaders are going to win. In their areas of leadership, good things will happen. When we notice them, are we celebrating the wins with them and announcing those wins to the larger group of staff or congregants? If not, we should. As we saw in chapter 6, good leaders celebrate wins and not just organizational wins—individual wins as well. It's one thing for staff members to talk about their wins, but it's quite another to have the main leader see that win and announce it on a young leader's behalf. It validates the young leader and allows the whole congregation or organization to see that what this young leader is currently doing is valued and that the young leader is being recognized. If we only highlight the losses of our young leaders, we deprive them of the affirmation they need to grow. They will feel as if they can't contribute anything worthwhile unless we give them some influence by celebrating their wins.

Allow Their Voice to Be Heard by the Main Body

One of the most affirming and releasing things I've experienced was being able to preach at Allegheny Center Alliance Church. I was around twenty-seven. I had just launched our campus church plant at Pitt and was allowed to preach to our entire congregation of approximately three thousand people. I had to preach five times because our space is small and we have a large congregation, but I didn't care. I was being released and given the influence of a large amount of people. My gifts were affirmed, and I was validated as a person. I was able to share my passion, and the church as a whole was able to hear my ideas and calling for the campus plant. I was and have been blessed by that as well as many other opportunities to preach at my home church.

I don't think I could've articulated then what it meant to me, but I know I felt released into a new season of leadership in their allowance of me speaking to the whole church. That was a crucial moment in my development as a pastor and as a young leader. I think it has benefited the church as well to hear a younger voice from time to time and see that even some young leaders have a deep passion for God and God's Word (because the information on millennials causes many older people to feel that all young adults throw the relevancy of the Scriptures out the window, which isn't true). I was given influence, and I grew as a result. People in our church were able to get to know me in ways they never could before, and it felt validating to know these people cared about what God was doing in my life as a pastor on a university campus.

As leaders, we must find ways to give our younger leaders a voice in front of the whole organization or church. Their voice matters and letting them speak proves it, not only to the young leaders themselves, but also to the older generations of followers in our churches or organizations. Those who are in the older generations need to get used to a young leader being influential in their lives, and it won't happen unless the young leader is given a voice before those in our congregations or organizations who are a part of the older generations.

Speak Highly of Them

One of the most honoring, encouraging, and empowering occurrences came when my writing mentor agreed to do the foreword for my previous book, *What Good Is Jesus?* Warren Bird wrote this in his foreword.

> He's on staff in a 140-plus year old multigenerational church and he speaks widely to others leading student and millennial ministries. Plus for many years, he's coached me in understanding his generation, which is why I was honored to write this Foreword.[59]

When I read those words, I felt more than validated. I felt in many ways that as an author I had arrived. Warren means a lot to me and is a prolific writer, so for him to say something of this nature about me, in a public forum such as a foreword to a book, I was blown away. To this day, he still blesses my life with encouragement and challenge.

Due to our influence as leaders, when we speak highly of young leaders in *any* setting, we are lending them our influence and declaring they have something we (the church or organization) need. When we as influential leaders lend our influence in this way, those in the millennial and Z generations feel validated, encouraged, and empowered. It helps alleviate some doubt they may feel about their capabilities or calling. Those under our influence also begin to see the young leaders as someone to follow.

I saw this in my own life just recently. Although he is now a friend of mine, he respected me before he knew me due to Warren's foreword in my book. Dan Boal, the national youth director of my denomination (The Christian and Missionary Alliance) hadn't yet met me, but agreed to read my book, largely due to

Warren speaking highly of it. Dan told me when we met: "Having Warren write your foreword, that's a big deal, man!" I agreed and was again reminded that influence can encourage others to follow you or listen to your voice. I believe Dan and I would've been friends despite this, but I had immediate influence with him because I was spoken highly of by a person of influence.

I can't underscore enough the importance of this for young leaders. This form of lending influence is virtually cost-free to your influence cash account as well. Sure, if my book was awful or was just plain unreadable, Warren may have gotten sideways looks for supporting it, but those sideways looks would *never* cause him to lose his influence because of his impeccable track record. Speaking highly of young leaders when they succeed doesn't take cash out of your account either. Rather, I would argue it *adds* cash in your influence account because a young leader on the rise with your recommendation makes you look good. If you had a part in that growth, some of that success will be attributed to you and your influence in the young leader's life. Many young leaders would wear your influence on their lives as a badge of honor. Not all young leaders will do this, but I guarantee many will.

I'm proud to say I am a product of many great men and women who have poured themselves into me over many years. I've already mentioned some of them, and others I have not. I am the leader I am today due to their influence on my life, and I have been encouraged by their speaking well of me. I have influence in many of the circles I am in due to their influential and public encouragement of me.

Release Dreams That Align with Organizational Vision

Earlier on in the book, I discussed dreams, voices, and failures. I mentioned slightly the importance of allowing young leaders to dream and then, if possible, helping them make the dream happen. This is part of giving influence. As leaders, our dreams and visions are not the only ones that matter. The young leaders in our midst also have a passion for our churches and organizations. Due to their passion, they will dream and have vision; this is just natural for any leader. So, when we can help bring about a dream or a vision—so long as it fits the church or organizational vision—we should. It's one thing to let young leaders dream and cast vision with you. It's quite another to release them to develop their dreams or visions. Naturally, this releasing must come with discernment, prayer, and much consideration, but I still feel it is necessary in order to make a young leader really capable of flying the nest into a more significant role of leadership.

This by far is the riskiest form of giving influence. It's not just one meeting, one sermon, or one team. Giving them the ability to release their vision or dream has the potential to affect the entire church or organization. If their vision or dream flops or falls on deaf ears, your leadership credibility could be in trouble. If your influence bank account is low, you may not even want to attempt this because it could bankrupt your influence bank account. Another quick realization you will come to is that this is not possible for every young leader who comes through your organization. This takes a selection process, which comes through knowing. When you equip them and feel they are ready and up to this type of pressurized task, I highly encourage you to release them to do so. Every context will be different as to how this can come to fruition, but I think it is a very valuable tool in the tool belt of any leader to cast a vision under the caring eye of a sage leader who can help grow that person.

Why Give Influence?

Maybe as you've been reading this chapter, you've asked yourself the question *why*. Why do the emerging generations need *my* influence? Why can't they just live off their own influence? Why can't they earn their own influence? Why do I have to stick my neck out for a young leader when no one was willing to do this for me? Doesn't this just once again perpetuate the problem of entitlement within my young emerging leaders?

The first "why" is *because it will give you (and your organization or church) insight into the type of leaders they will be once they have more influence and authority*. This type of understanding can be very insightful either way. You may see they are the leaders you've been grooming them to be or you may find they are not the leaders you thought they were. Watching how they handle influence will give you more insight into if or when you should hand off leadership roles over to them. This window into their leadership will help you better frame up timing for release. They may be more ready than you thought they were or less ready than you expected. Watching how they handle a larger dose of influence will give you this picture in sharper clarity.

The second "why" is *because it teaches them how to handle influence and authority*. It gives them a peek inside themselves. It will help them pinpoint areas of weakness or strength they were unaware of. It is a safe training ground for them to wield influence, so they have a better understanding of their own influence and authority when they are in full control as a leader of a department, leader of a specific ministry (such as a youth ministry), lead pastor, or leader of an organization. In moments of triumph or failure, you can help give them the tools to recover, retool, or redo what they did with their influence.

The third "why" is *because young leaders need influence*. With all the data that has been compiled about those in the millennial and Z generations, much of the negative press on the emerging generations is widespread. Millennials in many places are looked at as a joke, and I find this to be true even more so in the church. In 2016, Watermark Church held a leadership conference. To open up the talk on millennials, Micah Tyler designed a parody music video titled, "Gotta Love Millennials."[60] For the conference, it was purposed to show how many feel and think about millennials and then leverage those false dichotomies with a talk on how millennials have a powerful place in the future of church leadership. The description on the YouTube page states this: "This video was a parody that opened a talk at the Church Leaders Conference encouraging people to see past the stereotypes and recognizing the unique potential that millennials have!"[61]

The problem is this: the point of the video was lost to the general public and was touted for a time as an ode to the generation. In many church circles, it perpetuated and put lyrics to how many boomer and even Xer leaders felt about millennials. I saw Facebook posts by church leaders stating, "Oh, this video is right on." I hated this response to a parody, seeking to point out the silliness in lumping all millennials into those baskets. This is just one example of how many in the emerging generations are looked down upon with disdain. I know this is not true everywhere, but there is enough traction to make young leaders need as much influence as they can get from older leaders, just so they can be taken seriously.

Another reason why leaders in the millennial and Z generations need our influence is *because many think they will be the "lost generation."* I hear constantly about how the church is in a rough place for the future. I've been told that many churches are going to die because millennials just won't go to church. There is just an overarching sense of defeatism when it comes to the coming generations. Being an older millennial, I've also heard people say, "You're unlike many in your generation, and we like that about you. You work hard and don't act like other millennials." I know these are true, heartfelt words spoken by these people in my life. The fact that they are so convinced they are true is what causes me to sound the alarm on younger generations *needing* your influence. Many of our emerging leaders are going to have a tough time being taken seriously, and it is our job to help them start with more influence and more capacity than many think they are capable of.

When I develop a young leader from our church at Pitt, my goal is to develop such a strong young leader that churches immediately recognize that person as a spiritual and powerful leader whom they need to recruit right away. As I invest in them, my hope is that when they graduate and become a part of a church, they will seek to be elders, deacons, or worship leaders in their congregations. My hope is that they will be strong and confident enough to lead and lead well in those areas. They are the future of the churches they will attend. Even though I only have two-and-a-half years with them, I hope to transfer as much influence and training into their lives as I can, so they can blow away the expectations that many church leaders will have of them. To be unleashed with the best possible chance of success, these young leaders will *need* some of our influence.

What about perpetuating the systemic problem of entitlement within these younger generations? I acknowledge that this may happen when we lend or give our influence to the younger generation. The data and views of millennials in particular are not all wrong. Some of these truths about the upcoming generations will have to be worked on, called out, and retooled. I'm not dismissing that. However, we must not let those issues deter us from seeking their best. We must not allow those issues to cause us to be so biased against them that we do not help them grow. We cannot allow those issues to stymie the future of the church. This is why *knowing* our young leaders must come *before* anything else.

I'm encouraged by the approach Burlap takes with all the data on those in the millennial and Z generations. We acknowledge the real issues hindering those young folks, but we also purposefully point out the incredible data many overlook. One of those data pieces Burlap likes to highlight is that millennials are better with their money than boomers or Xers, which includes being generous.[62] This refocus on the positive capacities of millennials is one of the many reasons I choose to work with and write for Burlap.

I hope you see the necessity of your influence both upon and given to your young leaders. I hope you are inspired to move forward with your young leaders. Ultimately, too, I want you to recapture hope for the future of your church or organization. Have a hopeful expectation for the future. After all, God is still God, and God will be God when you and I are gone. If we trust God, we should trust God's children with the future. We have the awesome opportunity to develop these young leaders and hand off the future to them. They need us, and we need them. When we give them our influence, we are helping them have an easier run and a better chance at success.

CHAPTER 11

HANDING OFF THE KEYS

I REMEMBER WHEN I WAS FIRST LEARNING TO DRIVE. My dad had a green 1999 Honda Civic with manual transmission. I was petrified to learn how to drive without an automatic transmission. Yet my dad said to me, "If you can learn on a stick, you can drive anything." So, I acquiesced to his request. My father in his great wisdom decided I needed to learn on flat ground first, so we went to what's affectionately known as the Bottoms of Mckees Rocks, Pennsylvania. He handed me the keys, and I figured it out quickly. My confidence soared. I thought I was ready for the open road, but my dad wasn't sure yet. We had to do the manual transmission "hill test." I'm sure if you drive a stick, you know what this means. We went to a cemetery with a massive hill. My dad drove up this hill and went to the very top, just close to the crest. He put the emergency brake on, turned off the car, and handed me the keys. In my arrogance, I had no idea why this was supposed to be tough, so I grabbed the keys, turned on the car, put off the emergency brake, and proceeded to drive backward down the hill. I panicked and had no idea what I was supposed to do. Right before I hit a tombstone, my dad yanked the emergency brake. The car came to a halt and immediately stalled.

I sat there in the car, shocked. I had almost ruined the car and someone's grave. I realized I truly wasn't ready for the open road. What if that were the top of a hill with a car behind me? Pittsburgh is *full* of hills, so it would've been inevitable to have that exact scenario happen. I was grateful for my dad's quick reflexes and told him I wanted to go home and take a break from the car for a while. He refused to let me quit. He drove the car right back to the top, stopped the car, and handed me the keys again right away. He told me to ease off the clutch while my foot was still on the brake, and when I felt it about to catch, I hit the gas. I stalled the car out again a few times, but never came close to a tombstone again. Even after I almost ruined his car, my dad still gave the keys back to me.

This story is a perfect illustration of where I want to go in this chapter. The old adage—"I do, you watch, you do, I watch, and then you just do"—is a strong, long-lasting ideology because it works. All throughout this book, the majority of what we've discussed is "I do, you watch." There are parts of "you do, I watch" within the chapters previous to this one, but not much. This aspect of releasing is a gigantic leap forward because it is hard to let someone else steer something of such value to you. My dad's car was fairly new when I began to drive. It wasn't yet paid off, and it was his only form of transportation. Even with all of that, he felt it worthwhile to hand me the keys. I had to learn how to drive. He didn't want to be my mode of transportation when I could drive myself.

Leadership is the same way. We can't drive our young leaders around forever. We must release them to learn how to drive on their own. Many older leaders have spent years developing the churches or organizations they are a part of. They are precious parts of their heart. Their identity may be tied into the very church or organization they were called to lead because they've been doing it so long. Maybe that's your story. Maybe not. The truth remains—there comes a time to hand over the keys.

The handoff must be a decision born out of prayer and discernment. It is not something to be taken lightly. As a leader of leaders, that idea is nothing new to you. However, because many leaders are so well-established in their places of leadership, they fail to recognize the proper time for a handoff. This can be just as dangerous as a quarterback missing the timing with his running back. Behind the line of scrimmage, tackles, fumbles, sacks, and other types of turnovers can happen when the timing is off. The same is true in leadership. By failing to hand off the keys, you hinder a young leader's growth. By failing to hand off the keys, you hinder your growth. By failing to hand off the keys, you hinder the growth of your organization. I never would've been prepared to drive my dad's car on the open road if he never gave me the keys. Eventually, the keys would've been in my possession, but I would've had no idea what to do. This is why it is critical to hand over the keys, and at the right time.

As we move forward in this chapter, I want to give key insights on *how to hand off the keys*, as well as *the dangers of failing to hand the keys over*. Each generation is different, and thus we must approach issues as sensitive and as important as these with a view of the particular generation and the particular person we are giving the keys to. Here again, we see the power of *knowing*. Knowing is the epicenter of all things millennial and gen Z. No one is going to hand the car keys over to a stranger. I hope I can give some insight on how to do the handoff well.

This is not a book about succession. I want to remind you of that fact. Some of the issues I bring forth throughout the book and especially here in this chapter can be used for a succession handoff, but it can have implications for developing a new ministry or changing the guard in an established ministry. It can also mean replacing yourself. So, how can we successfully hand off the keys of leadership to the emerging generations? The first way to hand off well is to be blunt.

Be Blunt

Nothing will cause more strife for you and a person in the emerging generation than guessing games. If you see a young leader ready and able to take the keys of leadership from you, be blunt and say so. Give your young leaders a heads-up that this is not only what you see in them, but also where you desire to take them. If they hear this from you, they can prepare and pray. Just handing them the keys without much preparation can be off-putting. It can disorient them and cause them to doubt their ability. However, if you groom them with the understanding that you are handing off certain leadership keys, they can mentally and spiritually prepare for it.

Another reason to be blunt with them is due to outside opportunities. If young leaders think they will never get the keys and drive the car under your leadership, they may seek to find a different car to drive. If you were anticipating handing off a certain set of keys to them and they end up leaving before you can hand them off, you will get frustrated; and when you tell them what you wanted for their future, they will get upset with you for telling them too late.

I had that second scenario happen in my life. One of my leaders wanted me to replace him, but never told me. So, when I took a different position in the church, he was frustrated at me. In the moment I declared my position change, he decided to tell me what he was planning for me. The problem was, he never expressed that until that point. It was too late. Don't wait too long to hand off the keys, and don't wait too long to tell your young leaders what you desire or see for their future under your leadership. Don't make them guess. Be blunt.

Assure Them You're in the Passenger Seat

When beginning the process of "you do, I watch," it's important that young leaders know you are with them. Much of the chapter on giving influence can be applied here. You are putting your influence cash on the line and giving them room to fail. The same principle applies with handing over the keys. You give them areas of leadership, and you share with them bluntly what you feel they are capable of and what car you feel they should drive. When you hand over those keys, they need to know you'll be there with them.

Just like I needed my dad to pull the emergency brake, your young leaders need the assurance you will be there to pull the "leadership emergency brake" if they get in a leadership jam. Being in the passenger seat gives you the same view they have, as well as the ability to see things maybe they're missing, due to the newness of the driving experience. Knowing you have their back (as we discussed in the chapter on failures) is key to them driving at their full potential. Assuring them you are in the passenger seat also assures your other followers. Your whole team will have an easier time adjusting to the young leader driving the car if you are there with them.

Don't Let Them Quit

Leadership failures can cause many young leaders to quit. Since many in the emerging generations have been told how great they are, failure has the potential to derail them. Many times, if they sense they will fail at something, they either don't touch it with a ten-foot pole, or during failure, they quit. Many treat it as if they didn't fail because they chose to quit, and that is how they deal with their failure. This is one aspect of the emerging leaders that we must deal with, but we can gently guide them to reject quitting. We discussed failure and how we as older leaders must allow them to fail. We must also help them *deal* with failure.

I think this is one of the many issues boomers and millennials clash over. As boomers or Xers, you dealt with failure and you pulled yourselves up by yourself because when you failed, either you got up on your own or you were forced to stay down. This is where your generation feels as if the emerging generations are weakest, and it frustrates you. Are they weak in this area? Yes, but your impatience does nothing to help them solve the problem. This may be the one area where I will say the emerging generation needs to be "coddled," as many in your generations would say. *Failure is inevitable, and the emerging leaders must come to grips with that.* You must come to grips with the reality that they speak a different language as it pertains to failure. The problem is that each individual millennial and gen Z young person speaks different dialects of the same language when it comes to failure. So, you must *know* them, learn their language, and speak truth into them the way they can hear it.

If you go to a different country and attempt to speak your native language to a person with a different native language, confusion, frustration, and eventually severe irritation will develop on both ends. Learn the language of your young emerging leaders; it is a foreign language to most in the older generations. Then and only then can you help them deal with failure. With that said, we cannot let our young emerging leaders quit after failure. When I almost wrecked my dad's car and he had to pull the emergency brake, I was embarrassed. I tried to walk away from the driving lesson because of my massive failure to handle the manual vehicle. Yet my dad in his wisdom immediately put me right back into the driver's seat with the keys, took me to the place where I failed, and said, "Try again." His belief in me and encouragement to keep going made all the difference. If we *know* our young leaders can hack it and we *know* they can succeed, we *must* push them to keep going and to get back up when they fall.

Don't Micromanage

Nothing is worse for a driver than a backseat driver. When a backseat driver micromanages a driver, it causes the driver to second-guess every move at every turn. If the person "directing" the driver persists, it will even stymie the driver's confidence. The driver may even get so frustrated that they'd say to the backseat driver, "Fine! Do *you* want to drive?" This is how many leaders act when they give younger leaders the keys. They become backseat drivers, which causes younger leaders to second-guess themselves. Their confidence gets stymied and they feel like giving up because it is just not good enough. I think this scenario could be used with any generation leading another. I'm sure it is not just the leaders in the millennial and Z generation who would get frustrated with this level of micro-managing, but it may be a more sensitive issue with them, due to their predilection for walking away from possible failure. Either way, if you give the keys over in a certain area of leadership and continue to sit in the passenger seat with them, your backseat-driver leadership will be detrimental for the younger leaders. That type of "unleashing" may slow down their ability to lead rather than speed it up. As older leaders seeking to release new, young leaders, we have to be for them and not against them. Micromanaging, whether we mean to communicate this or not, states, "I don't trust you. I wish I were driving because I'd do it better." To a young leader (or any age leader), this feels like the opposite of "having their backs." In my experience, many times an older leader's micromanagement stems from the style of driving. It rarely has to do with a large deficiency on the part of the younger leader and everything to do with the way the younger leader is driving. Younger leaders are going to approach the road of leadership differently than most older leaders. This is simply stylistic. They will preach differently, lead staff differently, and approach problems differently. We must determine if we are going after deficient leadership or a different leadership style when we seek to help a younger leader drive better as a leader with the keys. When we take time to think through this grid, we will be silent more often than we speak when it comes to "course correction" with our younger leaders.

Handing Off

Giving young leaders the keys may be giving them more autonomy in the areas they currently lead. It may be giving them a new position of leadership with more responsibilities. It may take the form of replacing another leader within the organization with a younger leader. Handing off the keys may mean your church or organization develops a whole new role so this person can lead to full capacity. Finally, handing off the keys may mean you begin the process of that younger leader replacing you in your role. Whatever it may mean in your context, there are younger leaders who need to be released to drive. If you remain in the car with them for a time, they will gain confidence as you encourage and help them become better leadership drivers. This is the "you do, I watch" part. However, there is one more step before the young leader is fully unleashed.

Getting Out of the Car

The last step in unleashing your younger leaders is getting out of the car and allowing them to drive off in leadership without you. You've handed over the keys. They are *doing* while you *watch* them, and you are right there to help bail them out of a jam. The final step is to let them go. This is the hardest part of my job at Aletheia. College students leave and graduate every year. Every year, I send out into the world leaders I've poured into for years. This past year, the president of our student organization and a fantastic church leader graduated and left to go to a one-year medical research program. It was tough for us to watch her go, especially because we thought she'd stick around after graduation. Another student who had found Christ at our church left school and went back home. I know from experience that getting out of the car is tough, but to fully release and unleash our younger leaders, we have to get out of the car.

Getting out of the car generally looks one of two ways. The first may mean recognizing their ability, understanding they've outgrown their current role, and then sending them out into a different church or organization where you know they will flourish in a larger role in a new place. The second may mean you stepping down from your current role and handing it off to the emerging generation leader. You allow them to replace you.

The biggest problem many leaders face about getting out of the car is timing. You don't want to jump the gun, nor do you want to linger too long. Many young leaders languish in areas of leadership, waiting too long to be unleashed, and begin to diminish. Some young leaders become so impatient, they make a move away from your organization that may hinder them because you took too long to either give them the keys or get out of the car. Still other times, an older leader may misread the timing and put younger leaders in an area of leadership they were not fully prepared for. Then how do we know the correct timing? For me, in many cases I have no choice; when the students are done with their undergraduate degree, ninety percent of them leave. With that said, I think three things can help determine the right timing—*knowing* the young leader well enough to determine readiness; *knowing* yourself and being honest with yourself on your current effectiveness; and *knowing* your church, organization, and people well enough to determine if they are ready for a new guard.

Knowing the Young Leader

This goes back to part 1 of the book. (Seems to happen a lot, right? That's because it's that important.) When we take time to really know our young leaders, equip them as best we can, watch them as they gain influence, and then sit back and see how they drive the car, we will be able to gauge their readiness with almost pinpoint accuracy. Fail at any of these areas with them, and we will miss it. Many older leaders think they know their younger leaders, but haven't taken time to ask the right questions or to release them in certain ways to see them lead. We can think we know our younger leaders by simply observing them, but we may fail to really capture the depth of their heart or even fail to ask them their desires. This type of false *knowing* could possibly hinder them and us in the timing of unleashing. Maintain the good question-asking. Keep listening to their heart, dreams, and desires. Take time to really observe them in their element; do so sometimes without them knowing you're watching. Ask others who are under the leadership of the young leader their take on the readiness of the leader. You may find your leaders are better or maybe even worse than you thought.

If you determine they are ready to either go to some new place with a higher level of leadership or to replace you, find a way to let them know that will empower them rather than hinder them. If you feel they are ready to fly the coop and drive on their own—that, for them, is to move to a different church or organization—make sure they know you know they're ready, and you're not trying to force them out. Don't put a time limit on it. Just keep encouraging them that they are now ready to take to the open road.

Knowing Yourself

As an older, established leader, I think it is wise to take a yearly step back and seek the Lord. When we've been in a place ten-plus years, we may no longer be as effective as we once were. Maybe we need to move into a different area of leadership or a new church or organization. Don't get me wrong; I'm all for longevity and believe many leaders are called to continue well past twenty years in a leadership role. However, stepping back and seeking the Lord is always wise. Ask God questions like: Am I still being effective? Is my voice still the one they need to hear? Have I stayed too long? Are there young leaders I should seek to develop to replace me? Then spend time listening. Also, listen to your own heart. Ask yourself: Am I still one hundred percent invested? Have I been too jaded by this place to be able to lead it into the future? Have I been stopping younger leaders from rising due to fear of being rejected by your people? Do I still want to do this?

These question, both the ones to the Lord and to yourself, will help you know yourself better. Ben Roethlisberger of the Pittsburgh Steelers has made it known the last two seasons that at the end of each year going forward, he will sit down and ask himself if he wants to or can keep going as a starting quarterback. This type of self-evaluation is critical to timing. Many older leaders are too afraid to ask these questions, and so they keep plugging along. Many stay too long and hurt the church or organization they love because their voice is no longer the one their people need to hear. Another way to determine this would be to ask people you trust this question: should I still be leading here? They may say you're silly to ask such a question, but they may also tell you that maybe it is time to head to a different area of leadership.

Knowing Your People

Finally, to determine the right time to get out of the car for your young leader, particularly in the area of replacing yourself, you must know your people. Are they in a healthy or unhealthy place? Do they still need your direction? Are they ready or not for a change of guard? Much of this will come by way of intuition and the Spirit's leading. Sometimes, in order to hear correctly, you have to do some reconnaissance. Take time to determine the pulse of your people. Ask key leaders in your church or organizational community how they feel about the readiness of your people for change. Do not base everything on these findings, but use them as additional information as you determine to know yourself and your younger leaders' readiness to grow and take the car on the open road.

Giving the keys over and getting out of the car doesn't mean you stop communicating with and encouraging your young leaders. You could be a resource for a long time. Be available for phone calls and every once in a while, check in to let them know you care and are still invested in their success. Being out of the car does not mean you're out of their life. You are simply allowing them to drive their way, at their pace and in their timing without interference. Be a wise sage for your young leaders, so when they come to you in tough times, you can leverage your experience and give them the wise advice they desperately need. Finally, whenever you can, publicly praise them for what you see God doing in and through them. Speaking highly of your young leaders, even after they've taken the car out on their own, will go a long way toward strengthening them and showing those who follow them that you see they're doing well. Know them. Equip them. Then there comes a time where you *must* release them and unleash them to do even greater things than you've done.

PERMISSION AND INVITATION—
AN AFTERWORD BY JOSEPH WIMER

For as long as I've been working with Marv, he has been teaching a class we refer to as "PSF" (Personal Spiritual Formation). This class is comprised of material that is intended to draw people into the deeper life, a life that is healed and transformed through vulnerability in community, spiritual disciplines, and entering into the process of grief. My first experience in this class was the first summer of my employment with Aletheia. I would lead times of worship through song, then Marv would teach the content, inviting people to interact when necessary. The one class that is burned in my memory is the one on grief—and I remember it so well because I knew coming into it that Marv was going to ask us to write a "grief journal," which is meant to document all the experiences of loss, hurt, betrayal, and wounds from as early as we can remember. I recall my internal resistance to this invitation to grieve. I recall desiring to skip out on that week. I recall going anyway with body rigid, lungs restricted, heart racing. I recall leaving the class to find a quiet corner of the church to put pen to paper, and allow the grief to flow. I wrote maybe seven sentences. The grief was not the flow of a river, but a stunted drip from a crack in a dam. Needless to say, I left that evening frustrated and angry with myself. I hopped in my car and, instead of driving straight home, took a couple laps around the city. I yelled. I cried. It hurt. Little did I know what had just been set into motion.

To be honest, to this day, I have not completed a grief journal. So, why am I sharing all of this? I'm doing so to emphasize the power of permission and invitation when it comes to leadership, something that's been impressed upon me during my time of working with Marv. Though I did not (and have yet to) complete a grief journal during that spiritual formation class, the significance of what happened then is that, for the first time in my life, I was given permission to grieve, to be angry, to be hurt. Not only was I given permission, but I was invited to do it in the presence of others.

We will all have different responses to these things; mine was, "This can't possibly be right." Others will have been waiting for this permission and invitation and will spill out fifteen pages of grief in no time. As I reflect on that time and my personal journey in discipleship, this is when my journey into restorative grief began. I started my grief journal, and the Lord has sustained me as God has led me into other avenues of grief. I sought personal counseling. I found a spiritual director. I have written songs. I have named the sin, shame, and sorrow of my life in the presence of God and God's saints—something I wouldn't have dared to do just five short years ago. But I was given permission, I was invited to be known—and that has made all the difference.

To Be Known, To Be Told

I recently experienced another profound example of leadership that is authentic and invitational. My placement at Aletheia Community Alliance Church is made possible through partnership with the CCO (Coalition for Christian Outreach), a wonderful campus ministry organization that partners with the local church to put staff on college campuses who then mentor students and incorporate them into the life of a congregation—what a beautiful mission!

At a quarterly gathering of CCO staff, the director of training and crosscultural ministry made an invitation to staff to join him in walking through *To Be Told* by Dan B. Allender. This book is one that challenges followers of Jesus to tell their stories in the presence of God and others, and to then reimagine and reinterpret our stories in light of the redemption of Jesus. What made his invitation so compelling was that he did it by sharing his own story of shame tied to his ethnicity, brokenness in his family of origin, and profound loss within his marriage—all experiences that beg the question, "Where were you, God?" A chord was struck within me, and I sensed the Holy Spirit saying to me, "This is the next step in your grief journal."

While it's always a powerful and encouraging experience to worship and learn with my fellow laborers, it's very easy to play the comparison game in a group like this. I often find myself asking questions like, "Am I the only one wrestling with deep doubt? Am I the only one still feeling crippled by guilt and shame? Am I the only one who feels like a fraud as we're singing these songs to Jesus? What kind of unrepented sin is cutting off the fruit of my ministry?" The list goes on and on.

However, for someone in a leadership position to share so boldly and so honestly, and to find that he is also a fractured creature of God's delight who is saved and being saved, was so compelling to me. I had to join; I had no choice but to accept this invitation, to be known and for my story to continue to be told. This time, though, it was not just with a best friend or a counselor who is sworn to secrecy. This time, it is with fellow laborers, with those who are leading ministries and discipling students. All along, this is what my soul had been craving. The compulsion to make my ministry appear successful to others is waning. I no longer feel the need to pretend that my prayer life and spiritual disciplines are thriving. I have permission to be weary and frustrated. I no longer brace for a shocked gasp or curt condemnation when I share my doubts about God's goodness, faithfulness . . . even God's presence.

I once heard someone describe shame in this way: "It's this thing that we're deeply aware of, so we assume everyone else in the room can see it too. This drives us to do whatever we can to distract people from it." It can be humor. It can be our posture in worship. It can be effectiveness and efficiency in our work. We all have our coping mechanism. We all have our image constructs. However, as Marv stated earlier, if the most shameful parts of us are known, then there is nothing to be held against us. This reality has given new meaning to the phrase, "Tell the truth, the whole truth, and nothing but the truth. So help me, God."

You Are Not Alone

I share these two brief stories to emphasize just a small portion of what Marv has written about, and something that has arisen time and time again as we have worked together and sat with students over these past few years. If I could sum it all up in one sentence, it's one that I preach to the students who have been entrusted to me: you are never as alone as you think.

Just as Marv first extended this invitation to me, so I have taken that invitation and extended it to others. I've become more and more convinced that this is at the heart of Jesus' own leadership. He extends the invitation to come and be known as you are, to "taste and see how good the LORD is!" (Psalm 34:8). You can't think or reason your way into experiencing the Lord's goodness—it can only be done as we are opened up more and more to him, as we allow him to delve deeper and deeper into our souls. But we accept this invitation, not to keep it to ourselves, but to continue to extend it to others.

Part of the ministry I do with students is sharing my wounds and pain with them (with discernment; they are not my accountability), something I first learned from Marv's example. The awkward silence or confusion about what their response should be is all too predictable at this point, and I've come to relish it. I can do this because I've seen that time and time again, slowly (keyword!) but surely, they are opened up to be known as they recognize they, too, are carrying burdens of guilt and shame, which have been fueling their own hiddenness and masks.

Leadership that gives permission to tell the truth and invites people into a community where they find they are not alone—this is what my generation yearns for. By and large, we're sick of the image-driven church. We're weary of "putting it on" in order to be with followers of Jesus, so we leave altogether. We want to be known (this longing goes beyond millennials), we want to know that we're not alone, and we want permission to be honest.

Recognizing all of these things deepens my gratitude for the friendship, leadership, and co-laboring of Marv Nelson. My hope is that you have taken seriously the gift of what he has shared, and that my stories are a testimony to this form of leadership. We can only be loved as we are known; we can only lead as we allow ourselves to be known.

NOTES

PREFACE

1. http://time.com/247/millennials-the-me-me-me-generation/.
2. For more about Burlap, visit www.thinkburlap.com.
3. Character: John 3:16-21; influence: John 14:12; vision: Acts 1:8; communication: John 7:18; surrender: John 15:13.
4. *Relevant* magazine, 87 May/June 2017, 26.

CHAPTER 1

5. David Benner, *The Gift of Being Yourself: The Sacred Call to Self-Discovery* (The Spiritual Journey), 72.
6. Chris wrote a book in this series titled, *The Garden Resonates,* and it deals with how to speak to, encourage, and turn into disciples those in the millennial and Z generations.
7. http://www.lifeway.com/pastors/2014/05/12/what-millennials-want-in-leaders/.
8. W. W. Wiersbe, *The Bible Exposition Commentary, Vol. 1* (Wheaton, Illinois: Victor Books, 1996), 422.

CHAPTER 2

9. Simon Sinek Quotes. (n.d.). BrainyQuote.com. Retrieved September 15, 2017, from BrainyQuote.com website: https://www.brainyquote.com/quotes/quotes/s/simonsinek568171.html.
10. Edgar H. Schein, *Humble Inquiry: The Gentle Art of Asking Instead of Telling* (Berrett-Koehler Publishers), Kindle Edition, 10.
11. Ibid.
12. Ibid, 19.
13. Ed Stetzer wrote a great article on this in 2014. Even though it's three years old, it is still very true today: http://www.christianitytoday.com/edstetzer/2014/september/how-to-effectively-reach-and-retain-millennials.html.
14. When I say a safe place, in my definition it includes the following: a place where no secrets need to be kept, a place where help is offered but not forced, a place where there is no judgment, and a place where there is no shame.
15. An interesting study done by the ratings research company Nielsen takes time to break down the myth that millennials are only about themselves. I think it's worth the read: http://www.exploremidtown.org/wp-content/uploads/2015/04/nielsen-millennial-report-feb-2014.pdf.
16. http://marvnelson.blogspot.com/2017/08/rob-bell-on-bible.html.
17. Many studies have been conducted. This is one example that cites books with similar findings: http://www.kon.org/urc/v5/mahalihali.html.

18. I go into much more detail about this course in my previous book, *What Good Is Jesus?*

CHAPTER 4

19. John C. Maxwell, *Developing the Leaders Around You* (Nashville, TN: Thomas Nelson, 1995), 61.
20. Ibid, 67.
21. Written by David Kinnaman and Gabe Lyons, based off the Barna Group data collected from millennials in surveys and personal interviews.
22. Written by David Kinnaman and Aly Hawkins, and includes some statistics to back up their claims.
23. Also written by Kinnaman and Lyons as a follow-up to *UnChristian*, where they found the statistics of their previous findings were still true and even higher in some cases.

CHAPTER 5

24. As quoted in *The Right to Lead: Learning Leadership Through Character and Courage*, 37.
25. Ibid.
26. *Personality and Individual Differences, Volume 50, Issue 5,* April 2011, Pages 706-711: "Millennials, narcissism, and social networking: What narcissists do on social networking sites and why." Accessed from: http://www.sciencedirect.com/science/article/pii/S0191886910006215 on Dec. 6, 2017.
27. https://www.better-sleep-better-life.com/insomnia-statistics.html as of Dec. 8, 2017.
28. Reggie McNeal, *A Work of Heart: Understanding How God Shapes Spiritual Leaders,* 150.
29. Benner, *The Gift of Being Yourself,* 69.
30. Steve Saccone, *Protégé: Developing Your Next Generation of Leaders,* 29.
31. McNeal, *A Work of Heart: Understanding How God Shapes Spiritual Leaders.*
32. I've given a definition of this in a previous chapter.
33. To fully understand this concept, read *Dark Night of the Soul* by St. John of the Cross. This article is also a helpful tool for understanding: http://www.christianitytoday.com/pastors/2015/february-online-only/3-truths-of-dark-night-of-soul.html.
34. When I say "thought life," I am referring to the inner, often secret life I have in my head and heart—the thoughts I entertain, but do not verbalize. Thought life, then, is the inner dialogue we have with ourselves.
35. To paraphrase Ron Walborn, a true mentor and friend.
36. McNeal, *A Work of Heart: Understanding How God Shapes Spiritual Leaders,* 115.

CHAPTER 6

37. Maxwell, *The 21 Irrefutable Laws of Leadership,* 11.
38. Ibid, 13.

39. McNeal, *A Work of Heart: Understanding How God Shapes Spiritual Leaders*, 95.
40. Ibid, 24.
41. https://www.merriam-webster.com/dictionary/calling.
42. E. M. Bounds, *My Utmost for His Highest*.
43. Notice I didn't say better or more important. We cannot devalue youth ministry's importance.
44. C. Gene Wilkes, *Jesus on Leadership*, 68.
45. This statement is repeated and proven throughout a book titled, *Teen 2.0: Saving Our Children and Families from the Torment of Adolescence*. It is a book describing the pandemic of extended adolescence and discusses the entitlement of the emerging generations stemming from helicopter parents who sought to give them everything.
46. Dave Munger, *Cognitive Daily: Cuts in movies, and their impact on memory*, 2008, accessed at: http://scienceblogs.com/congnitivedaily/2008/01/31/cuts-in-movies-and-their-impac/ on Dec. 6, 2017.
47. Wilkes, *Jesus on Leadership*, 28.
48. Ibid, 54.
49. James Allen, *As a Man Thinketh*.

CHAPTER 7

50. Maxwell, *The 21 Irrefutable Laws of Leadership* (Nashville, TN: Thomas Nelson, 2007), 158.
51. Ibid, 159.
52. Scott Chrostek, *The Kaleidoscope Effect: What Emerging Generations Seek in Leaders*, 27.
53. When I posted that statement on my Facebook page, it resonated with many of my millennial Facebook friends—more personal proof that it is true.
54. Chrostek, *The Kaleidoscope Effect: What Emerging Generations Seek in Leaders*, 27.
55. Wilkes, *Jesus on Leadership*, 19.
56. Ibid, 11.

CHAPTER 8

57. Saccone, *Protégé: Developing Your Next Generation of Church Leaders*.

CHAPTER 10

58. Maxwell, *Developing the Leaders Around You* (Nashville, TN: Thomas Nelson, 1995), 69.
59. Marv Nelson, *What Good Is Jesus?* 14.
60. Watch here: https://www.youtube.com/watch?v=hLpE1Pa8vvI.
61. Ibid.
62. https://www.cnbc.com/2017/09/14/millennials-are-more-financially-responsible-than-boomers-or-gen-x.html.